THE UPPER ROOM

WHERE THE WORLD MEETS TO PRAY

Daniele Och
UK editor

INVITATIONAL
INTERDENOMINATIONAL
INTERNATIONAL

33 LANGUAGES
Multiple formats are available in some languages

 Ministries

15 The Chambers, Vineyard
Abingdon OX14 3FE
+44 (0)1865 319700 | brf.org.uk

Bible Reading Fellowship is a charity (233280)
and company limited by guarantee (301324),
registered in England and Wales

EU Authorised Representative: Easy Access System Europe –
Mustamäe tee 50, 10621 Tallinn, Estonia, **gpsr.requests@easproject.com**

ISBN 978 1 80039 390 5

Originally published in the USA by The Upper Room® **upperroom.org**
US edition © 2025 The Upper Room, Nashville, TN (USA). All rights reserved.
This edition © Bible Reading Fellowship 2025
Cover photo by bohlemedia/pexels.com

Acknowledgements

Scripture quotations marked with the following abbreviations are taken from the
version shown. Where no abbreviation is given, the quotation is taken from the same
version as the headline reference.

NIV: The Holy Bible, New International Version (Anglicised edition) copyright © 1979,
1984, 2011 by Biblica. Used by permission of Hodder & Stoughton Publishers, an
Hachette UK company. All rights reserved. 'NIV' is a registered trademark of Biblica.
UK trademark number 1448790.

NRSV: The New Revised Standard Version Updated Edition. Copyright © 2021
National Council of Churches of Christ in the United States of America. Used by
permission. All rights reserved worldwide.

CEB: copyright © 2011 by Common English Bible.

KJV: the Authorised Version of the Bible (The King James Bible), the rights in which
are vested in the Crown, are reproduced by permission of the Crown's Patentee,
Cambridge University Press.

A catalogue record for this book is available from the British Library

Printed and bound in the UK by Zenith Media NP4 0DQ

How to use *The Upper Room*

The Upper Room is ideal in helping us spend a quiet time with God each day. Each daily entry is based on a passage of scripture and is followed by a meditation and prayer. Each person who contributes a meditation seeks to relate their experience of God in a way that will help those who use *The Upper Room* every day.

Here are some guidelines to help you make best use of *The Upper Room*:

1   Read the passage of scripture. It is a good idea to read it more than once, in order to have a fuller understanding of what it is about and what you can learn from it.
2   Read the meditation. How does it relate to your own experience? Can you identify with what the writer has outlined from their own experience or understanding?
3   Pray the written prayer. Think about how you can use it to relate to people you know or situations that need your prayers today.
4   Think about the contributor who has written the meditation. Some users of *The Upper Room* include this person in their prayers for the day.
5   Meditate on the 'Thought for the day' and the 'Prayer focus', perhaps using them again as the focus for prayer or direction for action.

Why is it important to have a daily quiet time? Many people will agree that it is the best way of keeping in touch every day with the God who sustains us and who sends us out to do his will and show his love to the people we encounter each day. Meeting with God in this way reassures us of his presence with us, helps us to discern his will for us and makes us part of his worldwide family of Christian people through our prayers.

I hope that you will be encouraged as you use *The Upper Room* regularly as part of your daily devotions, and that God will richly bless you as you read his word and seek to learn more about him.

Helping to pay it forward

As part of our Living Faith ministry, we're raising funds to give away copies of Bible reading notes and other resources to those who aren't able to access them any other way, working with food banks and chaplaincy services, in prisons, hospitals and care homes.
If you've enjoyed and benefited from our resources, would you consider paying it forward to enable others to do so too?

Make a gift at **brf.org.uk/donate**

thank
you
for all your support

Just as we are

Divided tongues, as of fire, appeared among them, and a tongue rested on each of them. All of them were filled with the Holy Spirit.
Acts 2:3–4 (NRSV)

No matter where we look, we can find messages telling us we are not enough. Advertisements proclaim the wonders of products that will improve our lives. Self-help books instruct us on ways to be better leaders, parents, or spouses. Social media posts suggest life hacks that will make daily chores simpler and our lives picture-perfect. With all these messages swirling around, no wonder it is often difficult for us to believe that God already loves us – just as we are!

By sending the Holy Spirit on the day of Pentecost, God demonstrated clearly that each person is valuable and worthy of grace. Tongues of fire rested 'on each of them' and 'all of them were filled with the Holy Spirit'. Not only that, but each person present heard others speaking in their own language. They did not need to change at all to receive the gift of the Holy Spirit.

In this issue, writers describe some of the many ways God demonstrates deep, unconditional, unchanging love for us. In cancer diagnoses, failed entrance exams and other life-altering experiences, God is present. God's love for us does not depend on anything we do or leave undone. The gift of grace assures us that we are enough — just as we are. Let us live in a way that gives thanks for this most precious gift!

Lindsay Gray
Editorial director

Africa-English edition   French edition

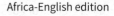

Writers featured in this issue of *The Upper Room*:

Ghana: John Adjah, Christel Owoo
Nigeria: Emmanuel Afolabi,
Muyiwa Benralph Olaiya, Dozie Ashiegbu
South Africa: Percy Mangwedi, Masego Mohlanga,
Lethabo Molotjwa

Gifts to the international editions of
The Upper Room help the world meet to pray.
upperroom.org/gift

The editor writes...

Some of them, however, men from Cyprus and Cyrene, went to Antioch and began to speak to Greeks also, telling them the good news about the Lord Jesus.
Acts 11:20 (NIV)

The Acts of the Apostles is, as the title says, the story of what the early disciples of Jesus – specifically, the apostles – did following his ascension. In particular, the narrative focuses first on Peter, then on Paul. In this respect, Acts is like much writing of history – it's mostly about the significant deeds of a select group of people, usually monarchs, generals, leaders and so on.

Now and then in Acts, however, we get a glimpse of people in the background of the story. They go almost unnoticed. There are, for example, the believers who sell their property to give to those in need (2:34), the many people who gather to pray for Peter when he is imprisoned by Herod (12:12), and the brothers and sisters who encourage Apollos in his mission plans and provide letters of recommendation for him (18:27). One of the key developments in Acts is how the good news starts to spread to non-Jewish people. Arguably, the first to take this significant step was not Peter, but some men from Cyprus and Cyrene who moved to Antioch to escape persecution (see 11:20).

These people are not the focus of the story of Acts, nor is much written about them in Bible commentaries or preached about in sermons. We do not know their names. Yet their unheralded lives are hugely significant. Antioch, for example, where those unnamed believers started to tell the good news to Greeks, goes on to become the base from which Paul launches his missionary journeys, and it is there that the disciples are first called Christians (11:26).

In all this we see that the real story of Acts is not about the apostles or about the unnamed other believers around them. The real story is about God the Holy Spirit, the Spirit of the risen Jesus, working through his faithful ones, great and mundane, named and unnamed, to bring about God's kingdom here on earth.

It's a story that continues, often unnoticed, in countless ways throughout the world today, a small part of which is told in the meditations in this issue. It's a story that I hope, as you read, you find yourself inspired to be a part of.

Daniele Och, UK editor

Every season

Read Ecclesiastes 3:1–8

There is a time for everything, and a season for every activity under the heavens.

Ecclesiastes 3:1 (NIV)

When my friend Ginny came to visit me in New England, she delighted in the autumn foliage. She had never before experienced leaves with such vibrant shades of red, yellow and orange. The brilliant swamp maple leaves especially caught her eye, so she gathered a few and preserved them to show her students back home.

While Ginny appreciated the spectacular colours as one of God's treasured gifts, often I have a different reaction. At times I miss the beauty of autumn because I'm focused on what comes next – winter. Where I live, winter means blustery winds, ice and nor'easters – strong storms that can deposit more than a foot of snow. Rather than investing in fully living in the present season, I tend to live with a heart and an eye turned towards the next season.

Today's scripture reminds us that seasons change, and each is valuable and purposeful in God's sight. Seasons can be physical, like autumn and winter. Or seasons can be spiritual, like those described in Ecclesiastes. Each season has its own merit and carries God's tender touch. Whatever the season, may we be fully present and alive to God's presence and love.

Prayer: *Dear Lord, thank you for each season. Help us to pause in the present and be attentive to you this day. Amen.*

Thought for the day: God is present in every season.

Lin Daniels (Massachusetts, USA)

God will make a way

Read Isaiah 43:16–21

I will recount the Lord's faithful acts; I will sing the Lord's praises, because of all the Lord did for us, for God's great favour towards the house of Israel. God treated them compassionately and with deep affection.

Isaiah 63:7 (CEB)

I grew up in abject poverty, and my education would have ended after primary school. But because of my passion for education and knowledge, I worked to save money to go to secondary school in one of the prestigious institutions in the western part of my home country, Nigeria.

Two years into my secondary education, I had spent all my savings, and my hope of finishing school was dashed. But then God brought people into my life who helped me through. The headteacher of the secondary school gave me a scholarship. Two American missionaries, serving in the town where the school was located, sponsored me and took responsibility for all my other educational expenses. From then on, I was able to continue my education through scholarships from different sources. Now I have several degrees. By God's divine providence, these three individuals raised me from poverty to what I am today.

Through my determination, focus on my goals and the faithful help of community, God made a way for me. Nothing is impossible for God. We need only to have faith and believe in God's promises.

Prayer: *Dear Lord, thank you for sending us helpers when we feel hopeless. May we support others as we have been supported. In Jesus' name. Amen.*

Thought for the day: When I support others, I help God care for them.

James Adetunji Kehinde (England, United Kingdom)

PRAYER FOCUS: SOMEONE WHO HAS HELPED ME ACHIEVE MY GOALS

Words of comfort

Read Psalm 18:1–6

In my distress I called to the Lord; I cried to my God for help.
From his temple he heard my voice.
Psalm 18:6 (NIV)

I have stage-3 breast cancer, and the chemotherapy treatments I'm receiving are harsh. I'm glad for the medicine, but it leaves me feeling sick, exhausted and in pain. I have worked very hard to stay positive for those around me, pointing to how God sustains us in times of trouble. But sometimes when people ask me how I'm doing, I want to shout, 'I'm having a terrible day! Everything hurts and I'm angry!' When I sit down with God, something changes within me. I can go to God angry and miserable, and God will hear me and bring me comfort.

Here is what I know. Even Jesus wept. Jesus had bad days: hearing that his cousin John had been beheaded, when his friend Lazarus died, certainly when he was betrayed by Judas, and when he looked out over Jerusalem, frustrated that his people would not respond to his love.

It's okay to have bad days. God understands our humanity and still speaks to us with words of comfort – at any time. We will have good days and bad days. God will sustain us through them all.

Prayer: *O God, comfort us and wipe away our tears when we are too upset to know what to do. Hold us in the protection of the Holy Spirit, and remind us that you have not forgotten us. Amen.*

Thought for the day: God loves me and understands me, especially on my bad days.

Kristen Lowe (Wisconsin, USA)

Recipients of grace

Read John 8:1–11

Because of his great love for us, God, who is rich in mercy, made us alive with Christ even when we were dead in transgressions – it is by grace you have been saved.

Ephesians 2:4–5 (NIV)

The woman caught in adultery was accused of breaking the law of Moses. Yet her accusers only condemned the woman without mentioning the man. This story reminds us of inequalities and injustices in our society. Women, youth, children and members of minority groups are often targeted by a society's dominant culture. Even in the church, we attack those who dare to do things differently. We have little patience for those who do not conform, and we are quick to judge and exclude others.

Jesus' response to the woman's accusers reminds us that we are all sinners and that although we have been saved by grace, we still sin. Acknowledging our own imperfections cautions us not to rejoice in the downfall of others. Jesus did not come to condemn but to restore sinners to a state of grace, and he passed on this ministry to us. God wants us to work for reconciliation in the world rather than judging others' sins.

As recipients of God's grace, we must continue to spread the message of freedom, motivating people to enjoy the new life offered by Christ. We do all of this from the perspective that we were once sinners found by God's merciful love and are now products of grace.

Prayer: *Dear Lord, help us to walk in the understanding of your grace as we reach out to reconcile others to you. Amen.*

Thought for the day: I extend God's grace when I am accepting of others.

Emmanuel O. Afolabi (Lagos, Nigeria)

Beauty in the fog

Read Jeremiah 17:7–8

You will keep in perfect peace those whose minds are steadfast, because they trust in you.
Isaiah 26:3 (NIV)

The weather forecast sounded almost perfect – except for the morning fog. Optimistic that it would soon dissipate, my husband and I walked the quarter-mile trail to the lakeside with coffee in hand and binoculars around our necks. But stubborn, opaque fog shrouded the lake and dashed all hopes of our seeing any wildlife. I complained that our walk was a disappointing waste of time.

Just then a mockingbird broke into song from the obscurity of the swirling fog. I listened to its serenade. And to the distinctive honks of Canada geese. To the splashes of fish jumping on the lake's surface. On our way back to the car, instead of watching for deer, we stopped to marvel at a maple tree's brilliant colours, at clusters of purple berries on the pokeweed and at a squirrel's treetop antics.

Metaphorical fog surrounds us at times. We don't know when it will lift, and our patience wears thin. But when life seems uncertain, it's good to consider God's sovereignty, to remind ourselves that nothing catches God off-guard.

So, while we await the lifting of the fog, we can choose to hush our impatient grumblings and look for traces of beauty. We can entrust our plans and the future to our loving God.

Prayer: *Dear God, open our senses to appreciate your blessings even when circumstances disappoint us. Your beauty is everywhere around us, and we are thankful. Amen.*

Thought for the day: I can look for God's creative work even on foggy days.

Esther Zeiset (Pennsylvania, USA)

Saved by grace

Read Ephesians 2:1–10

By grace you have been saved through faith, and this is not your own doing; it is the gift of God – not the result of works, so that no one may boast.
Ephesians 2:8–9 (NRSV)

I used to think I could gain God's love only through works and good deeds. I thought the more I went to church, served in ministries, and was kind and generous, the more I would be favoured. I thought I was worthy only if I did something important.

Our self-esteem often rises and falls depending on our performance and if people approve of us. This can be a real motivation to do great things. But when our self-worth is based on what we do, and we establish our value apart from God, that's when we run into problems.

Today's scripture reminds us that we are saved by grace through faith. This is a gift of God. It is not by our own efforts. We are all equally and abundantly loved. God gave us this gift of grace through Jesus. And when we focus on God's love for us, we are inspired to work joyfully for God's glory.

We love God, and that's why we serve. Our good works are fruits of our faith, not the source of it. Through Jesus' sacrifice, we can trust that we are immensely loved. We are blessed. We are forgiven. And we are worthy.

Prayer: *Dear heavenly Father, thank you for your love for us and for the gift of eternal life. Help us to seek your will and to become more like you. In Jesus' name. Amen.*

Thought for the day: God's love is a gift freely given.

Joyz Emarie Q. Sumampong-Albert (Davao del Sur, Philippines)

Looking ahead

Read Philippians 3:7–14

The goal I pursue is the prize of God's upward call in Christ Jesus.
Philippians 3:14 (CEB)

Several years ago, my father, a pastor for over 50 years, was diagnosed with a malignant brain tumour. The illness ended his preaching career, and it would have been easy for him to feel sorry for himself. But he did not. When he was moved into a skilled nursing facility, his wheelchair – and eventually his bed – became his new pulpit. He rolled around the halls telling everyone about Jesus. During tornado warnings, when all the beds were moved into the interior corridors, Dad would start singing hymns to encourage the residents and allay their fears. In many ways his influence was more powerful in his last days than ever before.

Some people believe their best days are behind them. The truth is, it's up to us whether our best days are behind or ahead. It's a decision we make every day. In Philippians, the apostle Paul – while in prison awaiting death – proclaims his intention to keep looking up, looking forward and expecting more extraordinary things ahead. Paul admonishes us to leave the past in the past and press forward to a higher calling.

God is not done with us yet. When we feel that our lives lack purpose, we can ask God for fresh, forward-focused vision and trust that our best days are ahead!

Prayer: *Dear Lord, help us to cherish our memories and be thankful for all that you have done. Give us hope for the future as we put our trust in you. Amen.*

Thought for the day: I will look forward to each day in anticipation of God's calling.

Rick McKinney (Kentucky, USA)

PRAYER FOCUS: THOSE UNSURE OF THEIR PURPOSE

Standing tall

Read Psalm 119:1–8

Anyone who listens to the word but does not do what it says is like someone who looks at his face in a mirror and, after looking at himself, goes away and immediately forgets what he looks like.
James 1:23–24 (NIV)

Until we moved to an apartment with mirrors everywhere, I didn't realise I had developed bad posture. Wide bathroom mirrors reflect my posture, and a big mirror by our hall elevator offers a last-minute check on my appearance. When I see my reflection in these mirrors, I pull back my shoulders and stand tall.

God's word serves as a mirror that reflects any bad posture I've developed in my spiritual life. I've come to understand that holding a grudge makes my shoulders slump with heaviness. Telling even a little lie keeps me awake at night. Reading about good spiritual posture in the Bible makes me want to stand taller.

That's why I read God's word daily and commit it to memory. That's why I write inspirational articles. Any notes I send to my grandchildren include a Bible verse or two. I don't want to be like the person James writes about, who walks away from God's word and forgets it. Instead, I want to reflect God's word in my life.

Prayer: *Dear Lord, use your word to nudge us into right relationships with you and others. In Jesus' name. Amen.*

Thought for the day: When I read God's word and apply it to my life, I stand tall spiritually.

Shirley Brosius (Pennsylvania, USA)

The prodigal son

Read Luke 15:11–32

*'This son of mine was dead and is alive again; he was lost
and is found.' So they began to celebrate.*
Luke 15:24 (NIV)

I grew up in a Christian family, went to Sunday school and church, and
believed in God. After a move during my teenage years, I made new friends
and my lifestyle changed. I left church and faith behind, but my mother
and grandmother continued to pray for me.

For 16 years, my life was filled with alcohol, drugs, huge debts and
depression. Over time I realised that this kind of life was destroying me.
I grew restless and longed for peace of mind, but I felt no sense of hope.

Even though I didn't realise it at the time, God's boundless grace and
love, along with the prayers of my family, carried me. Finally, God took
my hand and called me back to the path of faith. God freed me from all
addictions and depression and gave me peace and a new spirit. God
brought me together with other Christians who helped me come to
know God again.

The seed of faith that was planted in my heart as a child remained
deep inside me over the years. By God's grace I have been saved and
can now live a happy, faithful life, enjoying the peace and love offered
by our Saviour, Jesus Christ.

Prayer: *Thank you, gracious God, for welcoming your lost children
home. Thank you for your love and patience. Amen.*

Thought for the day: Jesus sets me free.

Freddy Kaur (Harju County, Estonia)

Amazing results

Read Ephesians 4:11–16

From him the whole body, joined and held together by every supporting ligament, grows and builds itself up in love, as each part does its work.
Ephesians 4:16 (NIV)

Years ago, my husband and I spent a week at a Christian camp helping prepare for the upcoming summer. Each person could choose a work assignment. Since I'm not a great housekeeper or gardener, I was happy to fold T-shirts for the camp's store. But our team must have been too efficient because by the second day I had to choose another job. I struggled through several tasks, volunteering to help cook and clean up. I wanted to be useful, but by the end of the week I was beginning to feel like my little chores (cleaning windows, hanging curtains, slicing potatoes) were insignificant. Yet on the last day, when I looked at all the work we had done that week, I was amazed at the results. A staircase had been built, the dock repaired, planters filled, the swimming pool drained and refilled, and the whole camp cleaned up.

No matter what part we play, we are important to God's work. God does not ask us to do someone else's part – only our own.

Prayer: *Creator God, we want to be a part of your mission to offer guidance and love to your children. Give us strength to accomplish the work you have for each of us. Amen.*

Thought for the day: Any work I do for God is significant.

Darlene Lunsford (Washington, USA)

The power of gratitude

Read Psalm 35:17–21

Don't be anxious about anything; rather, bring up all of your requests to God in your prayers and petitions, along with giving thanks.
Philippians 4:6 (CEB)

You can have some really valuable conversations over coffee after the Sunday service! On a recent Sunday, a young person in his late teens began to tell me about the challenges he was facing. He'd just left school and now had two career options. He wondered which he should choose, and he was anxious about what it would be like to study at a university far from home.

Then he suddenly stopped and added, 'When I'm all stressed out it helps if I turn my thoughts to gratitude. That really deals with the stress.'

I've considered my young friend's words many times since, and I shared them with my prayer group. It's a most important truth – anxiety and gratitude just can't exist together. The apostle Paul urged the Philippians to not be anxious about anything, but instead to give thanks. Likewise many of the psalms exhort us to express our thanks to God in the face of troubles.

Gratitude to God for all his grace and goodness to us expels anxiety. Try it and see!

Prayer: *Lord, may we practise gratitude to you, and in doing so know the easing of our stress. Amen.*

Thought for the day: Thankfulness opens me up to God's peace and joy.

Elaine Brown (Scotland, United Kingdom)

God's gracious love

Read 1 John 4:7–21
We love because he first loved us.
1 John 4:19 (NRSV)

My experience as a special education teacher has reinforced my understanding of God's gracious love. Owen, a student at a school for children with severe disabilities, had a strong attachment to me even though he was not in my class. Owen would race towards me and give me a giant hug whenever he saw me in the hallway. Because he was non-verbal, he never expressed why he was so drawn to me. I had never done anything that would warrant his attention. And even though there were times I had to ignore Owen's desire for my attention, he always ran to me the next time he saw me in the hallway.

Owen's unconditional and undeserved love for me reminds me of God's gracious love. There is nothing that I have done to deserve God's love and nothing I can do that would remove God's love for me. God's love is truly undeserved grace, just like Owen's love for me. Each time Owen reached out to me, I was reminded that God's love is a gift that I have not earned but have been blessed with anyway. Knowing this encourages me to love others as God loves me.

Prayer: *Gracious God, thank you for loving us even though we have done nothing to warrant your love. Help us to love others with your unconditional love. Amen.*

Thought for the day: God's love is the greatest gift.

Marilyn A. Wilt (Pennsylvania, USA)

God is present

Read Psalm 66:16–20

Blessed be God, who has not rejected my prayer or removed his steadfast love from me.

Psalm 66:20 (NRSV)

On 10 July 2022, after finishing my job for the day, I began my journey home. I had to get home to care for my wife, who was suffering from a fever. That evening it was raining heavily all over our city, and the ground was becoming waterlogged.

I was moving forward in knee-deep water, and trees had fallen all around. As I stepped over a huge fallen tree, I began to sink deeper in the water into a crater created by an uprooted tree. It was impossible to get help in the middle of the night.

So I called upon God: 'O God, save me. Pull me out from this crater!' And God answered my prayer. As soon as I got out of the hole, I remembered the words of Psalm 23:4 – 'Even though I walk through the darkest valley, I fear no evil, for you are with me; your rod and your staff, they comfort me.'

Prayers spoken in faith are always heard by God who can see us through any situation. If I am alive today, it is because of God's mercy and grace.

Prayer: *Gracious and loving God, we are thankful that you never forsake us. Help us to trust you always. We pray in the name of our Saviour Jesus. Amen.*

Thought for the day: God is my very present help.

Pradeep Diarsa (Gujarat, India)

A grace-filled response

Read Galatians 6:1-10

Be completely humble and gentle; be patient, bearing with one another in love.
Ephesians 4:2 (NIV)

Every time I saw that little red car speed into the parking lot of the coffee shop where I worked, I groaned inwardly. The driver was a regular customer who was always surly, rude and impatient towards us workers but sweet as sugar to other customers. Because she was a friend of the owner, we were expected to give her special treatment. I found myself judging her harshly as she claimed to be a Christian yet treated people so poorly. After praying about the bitterness I was allowing to build in my heart towards her, I was able to see her in a more compassionate light and began noticing her good qualities.

Paul reminds us in Galatians that a haughty spirit should be corrected with gentleness and forbearance, not by matching it with a bad attitude. Even though dealing with difficult people can be draining, scripture encourages us not to become weary in doing good. We aren't responsible for others' actions, but we are responsible for loving them like Jesus.

The church is a community where we learn to live like Jesus and attract others to him with loving words and actions. Such work isn't always easy, but we can help shape each other more into the image of Jesus by extending his goodness and grace.

Prayer: *Heavenly Father, help us admit our faults and extend grace towards those whom we find difficult to love. Amen.*

Thought for the day: Grace is the best response to conflict.

Megan L. Anderson (Indiana, USA)

Prepared for God's plan

Read 1 Samuel 17:32–37

David said to the Philistine, 'You come to me with sword and spear and javelin, but I come to you in the name of the Lord of hosts, the God of the armies of Israel, whom you have defied.'
1 Samuel 17:45 (NRSV)

The first time I heard the story of David and Goliath I was a child, sitting on the floor with my friends, looking up at my Sunday school teacher as she flipped through a picture book. The book described how a young shepherd defeated a giant with just a sling and a stone.

It wasn't until recently, while reading the book of 1 Samuel for the first time, that I discovered an important detail about David. Growing up keeping his father's sheep meant that David had to protect the flock from predators. If a lion or bear tried to take one of the sheep, David would strike the animal and rescue the sheep, bringing it back to safety. David was smart, agile and capable of taking on beings much bigger and stronger than him even before he faced Goliath.

So, it wasn't a fluke that David knocked out Goliath with one hit from a stone. In fact, God had been preparing him for this very moment. David knew he was ready!

Sometimes we may feel we lack the knowledge or skills to do what God calls us to do. But God prepares us for the challenges we face. We can take comfort in knowing that through the power of the Holy Spirit we already have exactly what we need to be victorious.

Prayer: *Dear Lord, thank you for the gifts you've given us. Help us to have the confidence and conviction of David. Amen.*

Thought for the day: God works in me and through me.

Katie Dodwell (England, United Kingdom)

Blessing others

Read 1 Corinthians 14:6–12
The Lord had said to Abram… 'I will bless you; I will make your name great, and you will be a blessing.'
Genesis 12:1–2 (NIV)

Our oldest grandchild is a senior in high school. He is a very talented young man. He plays the saxophone in his school's marching band, jazz band, wind ensemble and the symphonic band. He not only plays at school, but performs solos and duets at his church and other churches in our county. He has even provided wedding music for one of his teachers.

Naturally, we are very proud of our grandson. We are proud because he has been blessed by God with his amazing musical ability, and he is willing to share his blessing with others.

Many times God gives us talents and we fail to share them. We hide them and keep them to ourselves. Maybe we're afraid we won't be good enough and lack confidence in our ability. Maybe we don't have the courage to step out of our comfort zone. Whatever the reason, God is always encouraging us and wants us to use the talents we have been given to bless others.

Prayer: *Dear God, thank you for the many talented young people in our world who are willing and able to use your blessings to bless others. May our talents be shared in love and praise to you. Amen.*

Thought for the day: How am I using my talents to serve God?

Patricia Pace (Georgia, USA)

Capable hands

Read Isaiah 29:13–16

All of us, with unveiled faces, seeing the glory of the Lord as though reflected in a mirror, are being transformed into the same image from one degree of glory to another, for this comes from the Lord, the Spirit.
2 Corinthians 3:18 (NRSV)

Today I crocheted a butterfly. I found the instructions on the internet and followed them carefully, hook in hand. However, nearing the end of the instructions, I hesitated. Things didn't look right at all. Then I read the last line of the instructions, which said to fold the work in half once the crocheting was done. When I did so, I held in my hands a perfectly lovely butterfly!

It can be like that in our Christian walk as well. There is no denying it – sometimes life doesn't look at all as we think it should. The Lord responds to our 'corrections' in Isaiah 29:16, 'You turn things upside down! Shall the potter be regarded as the clay? Shall the thing made say of its maker, "He did not make me," or the thing formed say of the one who formed it, "He has no understanding?"'

The Lord's hands are capable. We can trust in his power to bring about transformation that will make our hearts rejoice. After all, the instructions are his and so is the skill.

Prayer: *Heavenly Father, thank you for the way you made us. We trust in your capable hands. Amen.*

Thought for the day: When I am in doubt, I will trust in the capable hands of my Creator.

Carol Westerlund (Uusimaa, Finland)

Trust in trying times

Read Romans 5:1–11
We know that all things work together for good for those who love God.
Romans 8:28 (NRSV)

One of the hardest tests of faith I've experienced was when I suffered starvation. While kept in solitary confinement as a pre-trial detainee, I was given no food for eight days straight. I cried out to God, 'How can you possibly use this to help me?' After my trial, I was housed with other inmates, and I soon understood how my painful experience had changed my perspective in a positive way.

In the prison cafeteria our food portions are small, so there is no shortage of hungry adults here. It breaks my heart to see the look of sadness on a man's face when he can't afford to buy more food to supplement the cafeteria's small portions. When I have money, God moves me to purchase extra food to share.

I believe God used my hardship to soften my heart. It made me more compassionate towards others who suffer from hunger. I don't always understand how God is at work in my life, especially during difficult times, but I have learned to trust that God is working for my good – to develop my character and make me more Christlike.

Prayer: *Dear Father, help us to trust you when we are suffering. Show us how to be more compassionate to others. Amen.*

Thought for the day: In trying times, God will help me persevere.

George T. Wilkerson (Maryland, USA)

Praying together

Read Psalm 130

I rise before dawn and cry for help; I have put my hope in your word.
Psalm 119:147 (NIV)

My church hosts a morning prayer meeting every day of the year, and we use *The Upper Room* to structure our time. We sing, pray and read the scripture. The pastor reads the day's devotional, and then, one by one, those attending share something from that day's message that spoke to them. After each person shares their thoughts, everyone says, 'Amen.' It is interesting to hear what impresses each person and the verses that are particularly meaningful to them at that time. The pastor then gives a message and often begins with, 'In the scripture passage chosen for us providentially today.' Finally, we pray about our church issues and offer intercessory prayers.

Occasionally, on cold mornings, I've found it hard to maintain this schedule. But it has become a habit before going to work, and I have been strengthened by it. Even during the pandemic, this meeting took place. And I take comfort in knowing that this morning prayer meeting will continue. The word of God will be spoken and heard, and the chorus of voices saying 'Amen' to the sharing of those gathered will not be interrupted. When we reflect and pray together, it is a rising fragrance of faith to God.

Prayer: *Dear God, thank you for speaking to us through scripture and the faith stories of other believers. Amen.*

Thought for the day: My spirit is nourished when I reflect on God's word and spend time in prayer.

Kaori Yano (Tokyo, Japan)

Temple maintenance

Read 2 Corinthians 6:14–18

What agreement is there between the temple of God and idols?
For we are the temple of the living God.
2 Corinthians 6:16 (NIV)

One day during morning devotions, I was thanking God for living in me. I thought about Paul saying that our bodies belong to God, calling the body God's temple. When I went to do my exercises that morning, I decided that I would call them 'temple maintenance'.

Words are powerful. Temple maintenance is a lot more fun when I am thinking about doing it for God than it was when I just called it exercise. Now I have not missed a day, except for Sundays.

It was a natural progression to start calling my morning devotions 'inner-temple maintenance'. Doing the outside maintenance is still a hard job, but I am hoping that as I continue it will get easier. The joy that I receive throughout each day from my glimpses of God and hearing the Holy Spirit speak to me are the blessings of keeping a well-maintained temple.

Prayer: *Thank you, Jesus, for the miracle of the Holy Spirit living in us. Give us the courage to tell others the difference this gift makes in our lives so that they can experience your love and grace. As you taught us we pray, 'Our Father which art in heaven, Hallowed be thy name. Thy kingdom come. Thy will be done, as in heaven, so in earth. Give us day by day our daily bread. And forgive us our sins; for we also forgive every one that is indebted to us. And lead us not into temptation; but deliver us from evil' (Luke 11:2–4, KJV). Amen.*

Thought for the day: Caring for my mind and body is one way of honouring God.

Paul C. Grafton (Pennsylvania, USA)

God's good news

Read Isaiah 52:7–10

*[Jesus] said to his disciples, 'The harvest is plentiful but the workers
are few. Ask the Lord of the harvest, therefore, to send out workers
into his harvest field.'*
Matthew 9:37–38 (NIV)

Years ago at an evangelism seminar, I met a young woman named Shanthi
who shared her amazing story. After hearing about Christ, Shanthi decided
to enrol at a theological college to learn more about Christ's ministry.
Later she started a school for young children where she taught them
Christian songs. When the parents asked Shanthi about the meaning of
the songs, she was able to share the gospel with them. Her ministry grew,
and with the help of the villagers she built a church.

Her story reminded me of the Samaritan woman who met Jesus at
the well. She was convinced that she had met the Messiah because he
told her everything about her life. She was overjoyed and ran back to the
town to tell everyone. Because of her testimony the whole town came to
see Jesus and hear the good news (see John 4:1–30).

Evangelism is about sharing the good news of Jesus Christ to help others experience the forgiveness, love and grace of God. Just like Shanthi
and the Samaritan woman, may we never shy away from sharing the
good news of God's love with everyone we meet – by word and action.

Prayer: *Loving God, thank you for your gift of salvation. May we
faithfully spread your love through what we say and what we do.
In Christ's name. Amen.*

Thought for the day: Evangelism is my opportunity to share
God's love.

Navamani Peter (Karnataka, India)

Give it to God

Read Matthew 8:23–27

'Peace I leave with you; my peace I give you. I do not give to you as the world gives. Do not let your hearts be troubled and do not be afraid.'
John 14:27 (NIV)

This past summer we had some old landscaping around our house replaced. The contractor did a fine job, and all looked well, but midsummer is not the best time to perform such work. The hot temperatures and scarce rainfall we experienced made it a challenge to correctly irrigate the new landscaping. I found myself wide awake one night, worrying about several of our distressed new plants. Was I overwatering these delicate transplants or starving them? After several exhausting hours of anxious prayer and worry, I finally fell asleep. In the morning, I awoke to a steady, soaking rain – totally unpredicted and unexpected!

I have been a Jesus-follower for years, but I still have trouble turning my concerns over to the Lord. My miserable loss of sleep produced nothing but a weary morning, yet God handled the problem – not only answering my question as to whether or not more water was needed but doing the work for me! Like the disciples in today's scripture reading, I am continually amazed by the way God answers prayer. The Bible tells us not to lean on our own understanding (see Proverbs 3:5). If we trust God with our eternity, surely we can trust God with everything else.

Prayer: *Dear Lord, give us the desire and the humility to come to you first, trusting that you will guide our way. Amen.*

Thought for the day: No concern is too small to entrust to God's care.

James C. Leyrer (Ohio, USA)

Jesus, our healer

Read Mark 9:14–24

'I do believe; help me overcome my unbelief!'
Mark 9:24 (NIV)

In 2020 I met a man who was recovering from a double organ transplant. He joined our faith community, but because of the fragility of his condition he connected with us primarily through online worship, phone calls and handwritten letters. Once a month he and I would meet to share conversation and Communion. He always marvelled at his healing and reminded me that being alive is truly a miracle.

I think of those visits when I consider today's reading and marvel at the restored life Jesus gave the child after his years of suffering. I am also amazed at another healing in the story – the restoration of the father's faith. After witnessing his son's pain since childhood, this parent's faith was wounded and needed to be made well again. His heart-wrenching confession, 'I do believe; help me overcome my unbelief!' led Jesus to have compassion on the father as well. He assured him with the faith-building words, 'Everything is possible for one who believes.'

When challenges wound our faith, Jesus meets us with compassion and a willingness to help. Jesus restores our faith with his healing presence and life-giving words. He makes it possible for us to believe again and to know with deep assurance, 'Everything is possible for one who believes.'

Prayer: *Dear Lord, thank you for your compassion in our time of need. When life challenges our ability to believe, help us to trust your loving care for us. Amen.*

Thought for the day: There is no wound that the compassion of Jesus cannot heal.

Donyale Fraylon (Texas, USA)

Spiritual treasures

Read Luke 11:1–13

Rejoice always, pray without ceasing, give thanks in all circumstances, for this is the will of God in Christ Jesus for you.
1 Thessalonians 5:16–18 (NRSV)

It's easy to pray and give thanks when things are going well – when we have a happy family, a good job or good health. But I've realised how tough it can be to keep praying and stay positive when I'm feeling down. At one time, I was experiencing financial hardship and had almost run out of money. I didn't feel like going to church. But as I thought about the fact that everything in this world is temporary, God quietly reminded me not to worry about all the things happening around me.

Our world is complicated with so many distractions, but God wants us to keep praying and avoid temptations. God also promises to provide for us if we ask with faith. It's okay to ask for what we need to live, but God is more interested in giving us spiritual gifts. When we pray and give thanks each day, we focus on our spiritual well-being. With God's help, we can let go of our obsession with material things and seek spiritual treasures in heaven.

Prayer: *Heavenly Father, help us to recognise the value of seeking spiritual blessings, and guide us to overcome our obsession with worldly possessions. Amen.*

Thought for the day: God has already blessed me with everything I need.

John Adjah (Greater Accra Region, Ghana)

Indispensable tools

Read Ephesians 6:14–15

God's foolishness is wiser than human wisdom, and God's weakness is stronger than human strength.
1 Corinthians 1:25 (NRSV)

In a rare unoccupied moment on our farm, I decided to repair a nesting box that was looking shabbier and shabbier each time I went in to collect eggs. The hardware on one corner was rusty, so I grabbed a screwdriver to remove it before applying wood glue and new hardware. I managed to loosen and begin the removal of the screws, then I thought to myself, *That's enough, I can remove it the rest of the way, twisting it with my fingers.* But the minute I put down the screwdriver and attempted to twist the screw with my hand, it would not budge. After a few more futile tries, I used the screwdriver until the job was done.

The tools God provides us – prayer, scripture, fellowship – are similarly indispensable. We often underestimate their power, thinking we have things under control, and attempt to live our lives without our spiritual tools. But when we do, we find life more painful and challenging with more and more failed attempts at overcoming the struggles. However, when we learn to use our God-given tools, we can more easily master life's challenges.

Prayer: *O Lord, we thank you for the tools you provide to help us overcome our trials and grow spiritually stronger each day. Amen.*

Thought for the day: God's way turns struggle into victory.

Laura Martinsen (Florida, USA)

Hardships

Read Psalm 61

*From the ends of the earth I call to you, I call as my heart grows faint;
lead me to the rock that is higher than I.*
Psalm 61:2 (NIV)

As I was growing up, my parents seemed to have a pretty good relationship. But they had hardships throughout their 22 years of marriage. Unfortunately, they separated when I was a freshman in high school.

I felt overwhelmed and worried about the future. I worried about what other people might think. *Will I be picked on for having divorced parents? Will people judge my mum for divorcing my dad?* Before the news got out, these thoughts constantly ran through my head. I knew my life would never be the same after. I never imagined something like this would ever happen to me.

Then I began to remind myself that God will always be there to help me through my hardships, through all my stress and negative thoughts. I also felt peace, knowing that the one relationship that's constant and never-ending is the relationship I have with God. Psalm 61:2–4 reminds me that God will lead me through this difficult time in my life. God will never leave us to fend for ourselves.

Prayer: *Dear heavenly Father, when we are overwhelmed with worry and negative thoughts, bring us peace. Amen.*

Thought for the day: Life is ever-changing, but God's love for me is constant.

Drew Bertussi (California, USA)

Made with love

Read 1 Timothy 4:1–6

Everything God created is good, and nothing is to be rejected if it is received with thanksgiving, because it is consecrated by the word of God and prayer.
1 Timothy 4:4–5 (NIV)

In Korea, all men must serve a compulsory period as soldiers in the army. I wanted to go to military school to become an officer, but I couldn't pass the entrance exam. I even retook the exam, but my score was still not high enough. Reluctantly, I entered a regular university, feeling frustrated and guilty for not performing well enough on the exam. Rather than studying, I worked hard to earn money and be a good son.

Then my turn for military duty came, and I became an enlisted soldier. During my time in the military, I met Jesus and was baptised. I learned about God who loves me despite my flaws, and the words of 1 Timothy 4:4 comforted me, releasing me from my feelings of guilt and shame.

When I went back to school, I was able to focus on my studies, and my grades improved rapidly. I was able to accomplish my academic dreams. We all are always loved by God and are never alone. God has now given me a new mission: to make the world better with the knowledge I have. Anyone, for any reason, can experience frustration and guilt, but God offers us a way to overcome these feelings through prayer and focusing on the promise of God's great love for us.

Prayer: *Our Father in heaven, comfort us in our suffering and pain. Help us to let go of negative thoughts so that we can serve you well. In Jesus' name we pray. Amen.*

Thought for the day: When doubts arise, I will remember that God loves me.

Jun Park (Gyeonggi-do, South Korea)

A new resolution

Read 2 Corinthians 5:16–21

Humble yourselves therefore under the mighty hand of God,
that he may exalt you in due time: Casting all your care upon him;
for he careth for you.
1 Peter 5:6–7 (KJV)

One January, instead of my usual resolutions about making more money
or losing weight, I decided to try something new. I read a book on gratitude, and I began a daily routine of creating a five-item list of people,
events and things for which I was grateful. Over time, my gratitude lists
grew to include more blessings – large and small. I remain a work in
progress, struggling with self-doubt and anxiety about my future. But
I have become less self-conscious and have opened myself to others,
offering a listening ear or a kind word. My outlook has brightened, and
my faith in God has been renewed.

Through prayer and Bible study, I am learning to abandon my worries
about having enough money or losing weight. I now entrust God with all
my concerns. God wants our fears to diminish and our hearts to grow,
increasing our capacity to love ourselves and our neighbours. As I accept
the inherent value that I possess and use my gifts for God's purpose, I am
renewed daily. Each moment I am granted by my Creator is a blessing
to cherish and celebrate.

Prayer: *Dear God, thank you for all that we have and all that we are.*
Guide us to love others and ourselves as you do. Amen.

Thought for the day: God calls me to love and accept myself
and others.

Jennifer L. Luckett (Texas, USA)

Remembering our value

Read Matthew 10:26–31

'Do not be afraid; you are of more value than many sparrows.'
Matthew 10:31 (NRSV)

Beside our front door we have a window box full of flowers in the summer and pine garlands in the winter. One day my husband mentioned that he thought a bird had made a nest in the window box. Impulsively, I went outside and moved the garland. A frightened mama wren immediately flew out of her nest under the garland, exposing five olive-sized eggs. I carefully covered it and went inside. We peeked out the window all evening, waiting for the wren to return. No chirping. No movement. Concerned, we wondered what would happen to her vulnerable eggs. I went to bed with a heavy heart, feeling guilty for causing the bird stress and the possible destruction of her family.

Early the next morning, I carefully looked to see if the bird had returned. I was thankful to see her wiggling under the leaves she had placed to shelter her family. We were delighted to see baby birds a few days later.

Through that little bird, God reminded me that even the smallest birds are valuable and how much more valuable each one of us is! In all of life's busyness, we can forget how much we are valued by our heavenly Father. When we are burdened with fear, we can remember that we belong to God, who tenderly cares for us.

Prayer: *Loving God, we give thanks for your tender care.*
Help us to value all of your creation just as you value us. Amen.

Thought for the day: I am worth more to God than I can comprehend.

Kathern Nemec (Ohio, USA)

The dark valley

Read Psalm 30

Lord my God, I called to you for help, and you healed me.
Psalm 30:2 (NIV)

In February 2023, I was diagnosed with breast cancer. Barely six months before, I had undergone a thrombectomy and angioplasty. As despair threatened to overwhelm me, I questioned God, 'Why me? You have just brought me through one health crisis. Now this. Why me, Lord?' In response, I sensed God saying to me, 'I will strengthen you with my righteous right hand. Do not fear.'

Enduring biopsies, scans and a mastectomy in April, I felt engulfed by darkness. Yet, Psalm 23 echoed in my heart, reminding me of God's presence even in the darkest valleys. Following surgery, I faced more medical issues and repeated hospitalisations. I often felt I was teetering on a precipice. Through this difficult time, my children were my unyielding pillars of strength. Their support reminded me of the support Aaron and Hur gave to Moses (see Exodus 17:12). I am deeply thankful for them.

As I lay in bed during those months, scripture was my refuge. Isaiah 40:31 spoke to my soul, reminding me of the renewed strength that can be found in waiting on the Lord. Today, I stand reinvigorated, echoing the psalmist's sentiment in Psalm 32:7 – 'You are my hiding-place; you will protect me from trouble and surround me with songs of deliverance.' God truly heals and restores.

Prayer: *Dear Lord, thank you for your steadfast presence with us. Heal us with your love. Amen.*

Thought for the day: God is present on every mountain and in every valley.

Nirmala Kumari Roop Singh (Karnataka, India)

Smouldering wicks

Read Isaiah 42:1–4

'A bruised reed he will not break, and a smouldering wick he will not snuff out. In faithfulness he will bring forth justice.'
Isaiah 42:3 (NIV)

It is easy to look at others – especially on social media – and think everybody else's life is sorted and we are the only one with problems. A lady new to church once confided to me that she had hit rock bottom and thought of taking her own life, but she sensed a tiny flame of hope within her that kept her going. I replied that once I, too, had almost been a 'broken reed', and I showed her the above Bible passage. Church friends had been a great support to me.

I am sure that most of us have had hard times when we have felt that we are like bruised reeds or smouldering wicks. Life throws up many challenges from which no one is immune. It might be a financial crisis, a relationship break-up or a health problem. It might be a significant bereavement, the death of a beloved pet or the loss of a good job.

Sometimes some of these events come together, and even those with the strongest faith can be thrown off balance. God comes to us then, in our time of distress, and whispers to each of us that he will not break off a bruised reed or snuff out a smouldering wick. We must trust this promise. We may feel broken and defeated, as if our flame of hope has blown out, but God is always with us. God will hold and carry us, and light our way.

Prayer: *Lord Jesus, when we feel broken and spent, please continue to uphold us and fill us with hope. Amen.*

Thought for the day: God's faithfulness is mightier than my despair.

Faith Ford (England, United Kingdom)

Divine connection

Read John 15:1–8

'I am the vine; you are the branches. If you remain in me and I in you, you will bear much fruit; apart from me you can do nothing.'
John 15:5 (NIV)

In this age of the internet, it can be difficult to go about life as usual when connectivity is suddenly lost. All communication seems to come to a standstill. This happened to us when our home internet connection was interrupted. There was a loud pop, and then our Wi-Fi cut off. We couldn't do any work on our computer or laptop. We had to depend on our limited mobile-phone data to complete our work and connect with others. Later we figured out that the Wi-Fi had been cut off due to a faulty power adapter.

Just like an internet connection, our spiritual connection with God can break down too. Unresolved sin in our lives can build up and make us feel distant from God.

If a strong internet connection is so important to our daily lives, how much more crucial is our spiritual connection with God! Without it, we can do nothing. We are like branches without a vine, a tree without its roots. But we can maintain a close connection with God by reading scripture, acting on our faith and sharing the love of God with others, especially those who need hope in their lives.

Prayer: *Dear heavenly Father, thank you for the connection we have with you through Jesus Christ. Draw us near to you, and help us to rely on you. Amen.*

Thought for the day: When I connect with God, I am encouraged and empowered.

Agnes Wee (Singapore)

Love your enemies

Read Matthew 18:1–5

'I tell you, love your enemies and pray for those who persecute you, that you may be children of your Father in heaven.'
Matthew 5:44–45 (NIV)

Walking to work one morning I took shelter from a sudden downpour under a bridge. Not long after, I was joined by a cyclist, who turned out to be an American who was enjoying his retirement by gradually cycling around the world. I asked him what insights his travels had provided. He pondered a while and said it was his experience that most people just wanted a peaceful life growing old surrounded by loving families.

However, he went on, there were exceptions. He shared a story of travelling through Morocco, where he met a group of nomadic trading men, including Arabs, Berbers and Bedouins. They told him of their sadness that trade between some tribes had ceased, because some younger men had taught their children to hate other tribes different from themselves. As a result, there had been clashes over territory, resources and religious beliefs.

We shared a moment of quiet reflection on the consequences of living in a world that teaches children to hate and to use violence, as we have seen recently with riots in the UK. By contrast, in the kingdom of God, the children of our heavenly Father are those who love their enemies, and the greatest are those who take the lowly position of a child.

Prayer: *Heavenly Father, give us the wisdom to teach our children to love, not to hate. Amen.*

Thought for the day: In welcoming others in Jesus' name, I am welcoming Jesus himself.

Jane Parker (England, United Kingdom)

No labour lost

Read Psalm 126
Those who sow with tears will reap with songs of joy.
Psalm 126:5 (NIV)

At an annual event that rewards hard work and excellence across sectors in Africa, our organisation won an award. I went to receive it. As I stood on the podium, the chairman named the feats we have achieved over the years, and the crowd cheered. It was a spectacular moment because the hard work we thought had gone unnoticed was finally rewarded.

Reflecting on that moment, I thought of the future time when God will honour the saints, the martyrs, the unknown heroes of faith, the peacemakers, the generous givers and others who work tirelessly for the cause of God's kingdom (see Matthew 16:27). Even when we feel our service has gone unnoticed or seemingly unrewarded, God takes note.

Realising that God sees my effort even when the world does not instils in me a fervent desire to serve God and humanity. I look forward to the day when I will stand before God among the cheering saints and hear God say to me, 'Well done, good and faithful servant… Come and share your master's happiness!' (Matthew 25:21, KJV).

Prayer: *Dear God, when our heart and hands are weary, strengthen us. Amen.*

Thought for the day: I will live a life of service, knowing God sees my good work.

Muyiwa Benralph Olaiya (Federal Capital Territory, Nigeria)

Listen

Read 1 Samuel 3:1–10

Then Samuel said, 'Speak, for your servant is listening.'
1 Samuel 3:10 (NIV)

I eased back into bed hoping for a few more minutes of rest before another long day began. My original plan to sleep late had been interrupted by an early summons to attend to my husband's healthcare needs. Although I am usually able to return to sleep quickly, that morning sleep evaded me. While I lay still in the pre-dawn quiet, I became aware of the caw of a crow, trills from a songbird, the patter of gentle raindrops and the soft sounds of breathing. Nothing exciting. Just restful reminders that God surrounds me with small gifts of peace and joy when I take time to listen.

The day's responsibilities still stretched before me. My body still ached for rest. Nevertheless, God's message of hope helped me rise to begin my day with assurance that I did not have to face it alone.

As Samuel responded to God in the middle of the night, I want to remain ready to listen when God speaks. May we never allow the busyness and bustle of daily life to mute the voice of the one who loves us beyond all measure.

Prayer: *Loving God, grant us listening hearts, ready to respond whenever and wherever you call. Thank you for the peace of your presence. Amen.*

Thought for the day: God who speaks also listens to the yearnings of my heart.

Diana Derringer (Kentucky, USA)

Scourge of the garden

Read Genesis 28:16–22

When Jacob awoke from his sleep, he thought, 'Surely the Lord is in this place, and I was not aware of it.'
Genesis 28:16 (NIV)

Filling the watering can, I became aware that I was not alone. Two large antennae appeared at the top of the can. Slowly but surely a grey neck became visible and then a magnificent shell, glistening and pristine in various shades of brown and cream. This scourge of the garden was a truly wonderful example of God's creation.

The glory of God is visible even in the humble snail. The appearance of the snail was just one of many occasions when I have gained a deeper appreciation of everyday things – when God and the wonder of human existence and creation made a strong impression upon me.

Jacob had such an experience when he awoke out of sleep at a place he named Bethel. Jacob had not been looking for this experience; it happened quite suddenly. Each day and in ordinary ways God's glory is revealed. Paying close attention to what is going on around us can be a transforming experience. God's glory fills the earth and skies. May we be granted the vision to see it.

Prayer: *Dear God, thank you for the surprising beauty of your creation. Give us eyes to see and ears to hear your work in the world. Amen.*

Thought for the day: I will look for the wonder of God around me in the ordinary.

Richard Emblin (England, United Kingdom)

Eternal faithfulness

Read Lamentations 3:19–24

The steadfast love of the Lord never ceases, his mercies never come to an end; they are new every morning; great is your faithfulness.
Lamentations 3:22–23 (NRSV)

This verse is one we can turn to when we feel overwhelmed, and I imagine overwhelmed is what Jeremiah must have been feeling when he wrote Lamentations. Things were the worst they had ever been for Israel. Many people had been slaughtered in a losing battle, while others simply died of starvation.

But Jeremiah tells us that he had hope because he called to mind God's promises. He remembered how God's steadfast love had not changed or been altered by the sins of the people. It was based not on their performance but on God's unchanging heart. Next, Jeremiah tells us that God's mercies never come to an end. Even though his nation had been defeated and the enemy had burned down the temple, God continued to be merciful to them. God hasn't stopped being merciful to us either.

God is willing to forgive anyone who cries out for mercy. Jeremiah tells us about God's great faithfulness. He had hope because he knew that no matter what was to come, God would faithfully protect and provide for God's people. Today, no matter what we face, no matter what has been torn down, we can call to mind God's promises and put our hope in God.

Prayer: *Dear God, thank you for inspiring us with your word. Help us to have hope in all circumstances. Amen.*

Thought for the day: Even in difficult times, I can rejoice in God's faithfulness.

Peter Caligiuri (Florida, USA)

Grow in faith

Read Acts 17:1–12

The Berean Jews were of more noble character than those in Thessalonica, for they received the message with great eagerness and examined the Scriptures every day to see if what Paul said was true.
Acts 17:11 (NIV)

After waiting three hours to have some blood work done, I went to a vegetarian restaurant close to the hospital. When I went to the register to pay, I placed the book I had been reading in the hospital by the counter. Quickly, the person standing behind me read the title and said aloud, 'Clement of Alexandria. How interesting!' When the person asked what had motivated me to read the book, I responded that I wanted to know how the ancient Christians expressed, argued and lived their faith in a diverse society.

The scripture for today tells us that the early Christians dedicated themselves to the study of scripture. They did not simply limit themselves to listening and believing what Paul preached. They 'examined the Scriptures every day to see if what Paul said was true'.

We live in a diverse society with a wide variety in the ways people think, live and believe. When we delve deeper into scripture and supplement our reading with works by Christian writers who faced great challenges because of their faith, the Holy Spirit empowers us to live and share the gospel. As Christians, we must nurture our spiritual needs so we can express, live and share our faith according to Jesus' teachings.

Prayer: *God of all knowledge and wisdom, guide us to your truth according to scripture. Grant us wisdom and increase our understanding, so we can bear witness and share your good news with others. Amen.*

Thought for the day: Daily Bible study will nurture my faith.

Vanerim Atilano Guadalupe (Maryland, USA)

Filled

Read Colossians 1:9–12

Since the day we heard about you, we have not stopped praying for you. We continually ask God to fill you with the knowledge of his will through all the wisdom and understanding that the Spirit gives.
Colossians 1:9 (NIV)

We live near the shore, and sometimes we go to watch the boats on the ocean. Of particular splendour are the sailboats. The wind billows the sails as the boats slice through the water, carving paths across the ocean. Without the wind, the boat just sits there, drifting at the mercy of the currents. But when the wind picks up, the slack sails rise and puff out and push the sailboat to greater distances.

Just as the wind fills a ship's sails, Paul prayed that the lives of the Colossians would be directed by the knowledge of God's will that comes from spiritual wisdom and understanding. That is what should be pushing our decisions, our motivations, our character – not our desire for power, money or praise. Spiritual wisdom and understanding tells us that what is unseen and eternal is more important than what we see all around us.

Doing what is right is more important than getting what we want, and pleasing God is where our true blessings come from. What the world has to offer will leave our sails slack and useless. But God's eternal truth can fill our sails and push us to greater distances than we thought possible.

Prayer: *Dear God, fill us with your Holy Spirit so that we may do your work in the world and follow your will. Amen.*

Thought for the day: Where is God pushing me to serve today?

Bob LaForge (New Jersey, USA)

The right conditions

Read Proverbs 3:1–6
*Trust in the Lord with all your heart and lean not on your own
understanding.*
Proverbs 3:5 (NIV)

'Sorry, Cindy, but the compost you were going to use is unsuitable,' the
school custodian apologised. 'The sunflower seeds will die before they
have the chance to grow.' Disappointment and frustration flooded me.
The children and I had been looking forward to planting our seeds during
our lesson, but we would have to wait for some fresh compost to arrive.
Instead, the children drew pictures of sunflowers and wrote facts about
their life cycle.

A few days later, when someone else was covering the class, I was able
to plant the seeds with individual children. It turned out to be a calmer
experience than trying to teach and plant seeds at the same time would
have been.

I thought about how often I have prayed for a goal or dream and
wondered why God didn't answer my prayer at that particular time. The
truth, I later discovered, was the conditions were wrong and I wouldn't
have been able to grow as a person on my journey. If the circumstances
aren't right, our dreams and hopes, like the seeds, can fail. Sometimes
God calls me to trust, wait or even change direction completely. I have
to trust and obey God. It is still a learning process, but I know with God's
help I can improve.

Prayer: *Creator God, your timing is mysterious but perfect. Help us to
trust and wait for your guidance. In Jesus' name. Amen.*

Thought for the day: I will learn to trust and follow God's timing.

Cindy Lee (England, United Kingdom)

God's best

Read Psalm 139:13–18
I am fearfully and wonderfully made.
Psalm 139:14 (NIV)

This week I am with my family in one of our favourite places on earth: Colorado. Surrounded by mountains layered in greys and purples in the distance, and orange and pink sunsets touching the horizon, I can't help but think about God's displays of beauty. And yet, God's biggest display is one I don't have to leave home to see – and one I often forget to notice. God's beauty is on display through the people God has made.

Human beings are 'fearfully and wonderfully made' (Psalm 139:14), images of their creator. To each of us God has instilled a part of the divine likeness so that in our uniqueness we can reveal something of the nature of God to those whose paths we cross: the weary woman in the check-out line, the man with his cardboard sign beside the road.

Today I want to ask God to help me to see the beauty in humanity, to believe the best of others, and to reach out and serve faithfully. May I never treat as a nuisance – or worse yet, overlook entirely – a person that God has counted as a pearl of great price (see Matthew 13:45–46). I want to slow down, look around and recognise God's image in every person I meet.

Prayer: *Creator God, give us eyes to see the people around us today the way you see them. Help my heart to love them as you do. In Jesus' name. Amen.*

Thought for the day: I will honour the image of God in the people I encounter today.

Anna Blanc (Missouri, USA)

Getting it straight

Read Proverbs 4:11–19

I instruct you in the way of wisdom and lead you along straight paths.
Proverbs 4:11 (NIV)

I was in a hurry as I pulled into the parking lot. I spotted an empty parking space near the entrance and quickly manoeuvred my car into it, intending to dash into the store for the one item I needed and back out again. But, try as I might, I could not get the car parked straight. After several unsuccessful attempts, I got out of my car to determine what was wrong. I realised I had been using a vehicle next to me as a guide, but the car was parked almost diagonally! Instead, I should have been using my side and rearview mirrors to align my car within the markings on the ground.

Even though it has been quite a few years since that incident, every time I think or talk about it, a larger lesson stands out for me: be careful whose life you try to align your life with. When we look at other people who seem to be successful or who are living a life that we aspire to, we may feel that we need to emulate them to achieve the same level of accomplishment. But doing so may lead us in a direction we don't want to go.

While there's nothing wrong with having good role models, we should strive for our lives to line up with the word of God above all else. When we focus on Jesus and pattern our lives after his, he will guide us in the way we should go.

Prayer: *Thank you, God, for your promise that when we pay attention to your words you will keep our paths secure. We pray in the name of Jesus. Amen.*

Thought for the day: Following Jesus' example helps me find my way through life.

Arlene Timber-Henry (St. Maarten)

We are God's children

Read Romans 8:35–39

'I will be a Father to you, and you will be my sons and daughters, says the Lord Almighty.'
2 Corinthians 6:18 (NIV)

Growing up, I was never very close with God. I attended church with my family, but I felt I sinned too much for God to love me. Feeling as if I was not good enough led me even further away from God. Sometimes I had baseball on Sundays, and without hesitation I chose baseball over church. Then I began skipping church, even if I did not have baseball. At that point, God was not in my life at all.

One night I broke down in tears because I realised that I needed God. I felt far away from God, and it was changing how I acted towards friends and family. So I prayed and asked God for forgiveness. I gave my life to Christ. Now I understand that no amount of sin could make God not love me.

God loves us so much that God sent Jesus to die on the cross for our sins. God loves us so much that we are called God's children. God is my Father, and nothing that I do can change that. God loves every single one of us because we are God's children.

Prayer: *Dear heavenly Father, thank you for your love for us. Help us to love ourselves as you love us, especially when we feel that we are not good enough. Amen.*

Thought for the day: Nothing can separate me from God's love.

Brayden Howard (Texas, USA)

PRAYER FOCUS: THOSE WHO FEEL THEY ARE NOT GOOD ENOUGH

Peace in the storm

Read Psalm 46
God is our refuge and strength, an ever-present help in trouble.
Psalm 46:1 (NIV)

As I sat by the window, raindrops splattered against the glass. The storm outside mirrored the chaos I felt inside. Uncertainty, fear and doubt engulfed me. I turned to the Bible, seeking solace. Psalm 46 spoke to my soul. How comforting it is to know that in the midst of life's storms God stands as our unwavering anchor, offering refuge and strength.

In that moment, a memory surfaced of a time when I had been caught in a storm while hiking. Lost and soaked to the bone, I prayed for help. Suddenly, a kind stranger appeared and guided me to safety. Reflecting on that encounter, I realised that God's presence is like that stranger – near to us and leading us through life's tempests.

I felt God nudging me to seek peace through prayer, so I poured my heart out to God, releasing my burdens and fears. I discovered that talking to God felt like talking to a trusted friend who listened with compassion and understanding. A sense of calm washed over me. God's promise of refuge and strength is a profound truth we can anchor our lives upon.

Now, when I hear the patter of raindrops, I am reminded of God's constant presence. Storms will come and go, but God's love remains unshaken. When we seek refuge in God during life's trials, we will find a peace that surpasses all understanding.

Prayer: *Dear God, thank you for your abiding love and for being with us always. Amen.*

Thought for the day: With God I can weather any storm.

Bella Mohensi (Stockholm, Sweden)

Firmly rooted

Read Luke 6:46–49

Just as you received Christ Jesus as Lord, continue to live your lives in him, rooted and built up in him, strengthened in the faith as you were taught, and overflowing with thankfulness.

Colossians 2:6–7 (NIV)

I studied the slender branch in our garden. My father-in-law had taken the cutting from his parents' blackberry bush and replanted it in our tiny garden. I anticipated sharing juicy berries with my two preschool-aged sons.

Approaching the garden, I inspected what I hoped to be the beginning of my thriving blackberry bush. No buds were visible on the delicate plant. As I stepped closer, something wasn't right. I wiggled the plant and, much to my shock, it popped right out of the ground! Upon further observation, I found that my sons had pulled it up and replanted it multiple times. The branch no longer had roots. Since the plant had not stayed firmly in the dirt, roots could not form.

Sometimes I get busy and don't pray or study the Bible, and my spiritual roots shrink like that of the plant. In Colossians 2, Paul encourages believers to continue to follow Jesus and let their roots grow down into him. When we spend time with God in prayer, Bible study and regular worship with other believers, we build our lives on Jesus. Only then will we have roots strong enough to hold our lives steady and allow the fruit of God's Spirit to be seen in us.

Prayer: *Dear Lord, help us build our lives in obedience to your will for us. Guide us as we pray and study your word. In the name of Jesus. Amen.*

Thought for the day: My faith grows strong when I stand firmly in the soil of God's word.

Sarah Schwerin (Florida, USA)

Red scribbles

Read John 5:24–30

Jesus gave them this answer: 'Very truly I tell you, the Son can do nothing by himself; he can do only what he sees his Father doing, because whatever the Father does the Son also does.'
John 5:19 (NIV)

My study Bible is filled with neatly underlined scripture passages, circled cross-references and handwritten notes in the margins. Interrupting these structured annotations are stray scribbles in red marker. I suspect my son added them when he was a toddler. He was doing what he saw his father doing.

Today's scripture says Jesus did what he saw his Father doing too. He did this out of reverent submission and obedience to accomplish his Father's will while also setting an example for us. To be a follower of Jesus, we must do what Jesus did. This involves obeying his commands (see John 14:15), being doers of his word (see James 1:22) and pouring what we've learned into others (see Matthew 28:18–20).

With Jesus as our example, we can continue to grow in faith and action as we imitate our Saviour. How wonderful that we have a model in Jesus!

Prayer: *Dear Father in heaven, help us do what Jesus did, following his example so that we may glorify you. Amen.*

Thought for the day: Today and every day I will aspire to follow Jesus' example.

Rick Stockwell (Connecticut, USA)

Never alone

Read Philippians 4:4–9

Do not be anxious about anything, but in every situation, by prayer and petition, with thanksgiving, present your requests to God.
Philippians 4:6 (NIV)

A mountain of debts had piled up, and anxiety and worry consumed me. I worked hard at every job I was offered, but still it wasn't enough.

One night, exhausted by the problems looming over me, I broke down in tears. It was then that I realised that for the past months, anxiety and worry had not been my only companions. God, who is stronger and greater than any problem I have, had been with me all along, waiting for me to surrender and seek help.

Whatever burdens we carry, we don't have to do it all alone. God will help us to carry our burdens. Challenging times will come, but when we recognise God's presence in our lives, we can make it through. The peace that we receive from God calms our minds and hearts so that we can surrender our worry and live for God's glory.

Prayer: *Lord Jesus, help us to remember and acknowledge your work in our lives. Lead us today as we live in service to you. We pray as you taught us, 'Our Father in heaven, hallowed be your name, your kingdom come, your will be done, on earth as it is in heaven. Give us today our daily bread. And forgive us our debts, as we also have forgiven our debtors. And lead us not into temptation, but deliver us from the evil one' (Matthew 6:9–13, NIV). Amen.*

Thought for the day: God is my solace.

Jether Ann (Benguet, Philippines)

Enough

Read Psalm 107:1–9

'I have loved you with an everlasting love; I have drawn you with unfailing kindness.'
Jeremiah 31:3 (NIV)

I once saw a woman with a tattoo on her wrist that simply said, 'Enough.' Although I wondered what it meant to her, I didn't give it much more thought.

After retirement, I began questioning my identity, my self-worth and my life's purpose. For nearly 50 years, I had identified myself by my profession – first, as an attorney, then a judge and finally as a professor. But when I left the workplace, I no longer knew how I should introduce myself or what value I contributed to the world.

Then I remembered the woman's tattoo: 'Enough.' My worth is not dependent upon the title I have or the position I hold. The Bible says that my accomplishments have no bearing on God's love for me. God's loving presence will direct my steps in all that I do. When I feel unworthy or uneasy about myself, I am reassured that the Lord loves me regardless of how well I am performing. And that is enough!

Prayer: *Dear heavenly Father, when we look to earthly accomplishments for our sense of purpose, help us to remember that in your eyes we are always enough. Amen.*

Thought for the day: In God's eyes, I am enough!

Sheryl Ramstad (Minnesota, USA)

Seventy-seven times

Read Matthew 18:21–35

Peter came to Jesus and asked, 'Lord, how many times shall I forgive my brother or sister who sins against me? Up to seven times?' Jesus answered, 'I tell you, not seven times, but seventy-seven times.'
Matthew 18:21–22 (NIV)

Several years ago, I experienced a deep hurt caused by a close friend's betrayal. The pain was intense, and I struggled to find a way forward. In moments of despair, I turned to the Bible for guidance, seeking solace in its wisdom. In today's quoted scripture, Jesus encourages boundless forgiveness. I realised that I needed to find the strength to forgive my friend repeatedly, even though the hurt lingered. I couldn't change the past, but I could choose to release the burden of resentment and anger.

I decided to pray each day for the willingness to forgive, seeking God's help in healing my wounded heart. It wasn't an easy process, but with time, prayer and reflection, I found a sense of peace that I hadn't known before. The path to forgiveness begins with examining our hearts and identifying lingering grudges or hurts we are holding on to. When we turn to the Bible for guidance, we can find clarity and direction. And praying for the strength to forgive opens us to healing and deeper connection with God.

May we all find the strength to forgive, just as God forgives us, and may this act of compassion lead us to a more profound relationship with God and a life filled with grace and love.

Prayer: *Dear God, thank you for the guidance we find in scripture. Give us the strength to forgive so that we can heal and draw closer to you. Amen.*

Thought for the day: Forgiveness brings me closer to God.

Dozie Ashiegbu (Abia, Nigeria)

Against the odds

Read 1 Samuel 17:40–50

David prevailed over the Philistine with a sling and a stone, striking down the Philistine and killing him; there was no sword in David's hand.
1 Samuel 17:50 (NRSV)

At the start of my freshman year of high school, I was one of about 60 boys trying out for the basketball team. Only 20 players would be chosen. I was one of the shortest boys trying out and did not have as much experience playing basketball as the others. I could sense the doubt that the other boys and even the coaches had when they first saw me.

Throughout the week of try-outs, I practised and played to the best of my ability. It was hard not to doubt myself. However, I tried to remember that God was giving me strength each day. I put my trust in God's plan for me, and I made the team!

Like David's story in 1 Samuel 17, I realised that we will all face challenges or obstacles that seem impossible to overcome. We may be discounted by others, but we can always trust that no matter what we might face, God is with us every step of the way. If God empowered David to defeat Goliath, God can also give us the strength to triumph over anything that stands in our way.

Prayer: *Thank you, God, for giving us the strength to overcome any obstacle in our path. Amen.*

Thought for the day: God gives me strength to overcome obstacles.

Matthew Fleitas (Texas, USA)

Clearing the way

Read Jonah 4

'He removes any of my branches that don't produce fruit, and he trims any branch that produces fruit so that it will produce even more fruit.'
John 15:2 (CEB)

The buzz of chainsaws and the roar of wood-chipping equipment filled my ears as I slowed my car to a halt. A work crew was lopping off big limbs of trees that had stood along this rural road for decades. Some of the trees were being readied for complete removal. At first, I felt sad to see these noble trees removed; then I recalled frequent power outages caused by branches falling on power lines or even falling on vehicles due to high winds or ice.

The pruning was necessary to keep the roadway clear and safe. Sometimes aspects of our lives need pruning to help us stay aligned with God's will. Like Jonah, we may not be happy about what God is doing. We may not understand the plan or the route to get there. Often I am reluctant to give up an attitude or habit that is detrimental to my faith journey or to others. Through prayer, meditation and study of scripture, we can come to trust that God is our protector. When we welcome God's clearing work in our lives, we can stay faithful and remain safely on the road we should travel.

Prayer: *Almighty and all-knowing God, help us accept your ways and acknowledge that you know best. Amen.*

Thought for the day: What needs to be pruned from my life to keep me on God's way?

April Bogert (New York, USA)

God's help

Read Psalm 121
The Lord will keep you from all harm – he will watch over your life;
the Lord will watch over your coming and going both now and
forevermore.
Psalm 121:7–8 (NIV)

At one time in my life, I was surrounded by many social and economic issues. I was stressed day and night, and it was quite unbearable. When I tried to handle the problems on my own, it only seemed to make things worse. I felt helpless.

Then one day I received a call from a man of God who asked me to join a prayer meeting. Even though the meeting was at a location far away from me, I decided to go. When I arrived, I was heavily burdened. I joined the group in worship and prayer, and as I did so, I began to receive peace in my heart and my heaviness was gone. I believe God led me to that place.

Jesus said, 'Come to me, all you who are weary and burdened, and I will give you rest' (Matthew 11:28). God can perform miracles when we think there is no way forward. We can trust God to help us in all our circumstances.

Prayer: *Gracious and loving God, thank you for strengthening us to face difficult situations. We pray in the name of the one who saves the world and whose grace is abundant. Amen.*

Thought for the day: God can lead me through any difficult situation.

Richardsan Rajnikant Christian (Gujarat, India)

Living in mercy and hope

Read Matthew 25:14–23

His master replied, 'Well done, good and faithful servant! You have been faithful with a few things; I will put you in charge of many things.'
Matthew 25:23 (NIV)

I like sitting quietly in the pew in our small church before the worship service. The sunlight filters through the beautiful stained-glass windows, depicting stories from the gospels. Long ago, such artwork helped people who may not have known how to read learn and remember the stories of Jesus. They continue to prompt me to reflect on their messages for my life today.

On a recent Sunday I was sitting in my usual spot between the windows illustrating the parables of the prodigal son and the good and faithful servant. I observed that in both stories the main characters are welcomed and embraced. One is forgiven for his past errors, while the other is affirmed for his correct choices.

I thought about how living to serve Jesus is often a struggle. We have to start afresh each day in gratitude for God's mercy and seek God's help through the Spirit to love God and one another. It isn't always easy.

Oh, how much I hope to hear those words from Jesus: 'Well done, good and faithful servant!' But I am grateful for the Lord's mercy and forgiveness that I see in the story of the prodigal son. I can seek to serve the Lord by also extending mercy and forgiveness to others in my life.

Prayer: *Merciful God, help us to extend mercy and forgiveness to others as we remember the mercy and forgiveness you have given us. Amen.*

Thought for the day: I will seek to serve God and be grateful for God's mercy.

Janet B. Edwards (North Carolina, USA)

God of surprises

Read Deuteronomy 31:1–8

The Lord is my shepherd, I lack nothing.
Psalm 23:1 (NIV)

I am serving time in a federal prison. I have started writing to pass the time, and I decided to work on some meditations. I have faith that God will always provide what I need – sometimes in unexpected ways.

One day as I attempted to write, I was complaining about the pencil I was using. The pencils provided by the prison are not good quality. They are flimsy by design to prevent inmates from harming themselves or others with them, and the low-grade graphite does not write well. I continued to plug along writing with the uncooperative pencil when a security guard walked up to the cell and knocked. I didn't pay much attention and continued writing. My cellmate went to see what the guard wanted. The guard showed him a pen and asked if he needed one. My cellmate took the pen and thanked the guard. Turning to me, my cellmate said, 'Here, take the pen. I already have one.'

For 40 days, I had been asking different guards for a pen. I felt this was God's way of showing me that even in the smallest of details, the Lord is aware of my needs and always by my side. And if God is by my side, all will be well, and I will lack nothing. I felt an inner sense of peace and comfort knowing that my life and my situation are in God's hands.

Prayer: *God of wonder and surprises, be patient with us as you teach us to place our trust in you. Thank you for the joy of knowing that in your love, we lack for nothing. Amen.*

Thought for the day: God will provide for me in real and unexpected ways.

Jesús Manuel Salazar-Núñez (Texas, USA)

Turn it off!

Read Luke 12:22–31

The Spirit God gave us does not make us timid, but gives us power, love and self-discipline.
2 Timothy 1:7 (NIV)

Years ago when I was young, my siblings and I thought it would be fun to watch a scary movie. More than just 'scary', the movie we chose turned out to be dark and terrifying. As it progressed, we were swept up in the story and gripped by fear. At one point, we all erupted in screams. Suddenly, our dad strode into the room, pointed to the TV and said, 'You know, you can turn that thing off.'

I still smile when I think of my father's practical wisdom. But his words ring true even today as I stare at screen after screen, subjecting myself to an unprecedented amount of news, information and opinions that mostly stress me out and sometimes fill me with fear. Fortunately, I am learning that I do, indeed, have the power to turn it all off.

The world and its problems don't magically disappear when we turn off our screens. Nor do our responsibilities. But when we turn our worries into reasons for prayer (see Philippians 4:6) and immerse ourselves in God's word, we can remember God's sovereignty and power. Then our perspective changes. In God, our hearts and minds find protection and peace as we engage with the world.

Prayer: *O Lord, help us to be discerning and self-disciplined as we navigate life in an overwhelming world. We trust in your power and love. In Jesus' name. Amen.*

Thought for the day: Immersing myself in God's word can protect me from fear.

Gail Parker (Maryland, USA)

Creator of heaven and earth

Read Psalm 19:1–9

The heavens declare the glory of God; the skies proclaim the work of his hands.

Psalm 19:1 (NIV)

For health reasons, I was told to begin an exercise regimen. The busyness of my daily schedule made this difficult. So after putting my children to bed for the night, I began to take evening walks. I made it a habit to listen to praise music or sermons during these walks, but it was also a good time to talk to God.

Each night along my walk I see the brilliance of the stars and moon reflected on the sea. The clouds and the sound of the waves and wind are a wordless language that astounds me – a nocturnal creation that brings me to tears. All this wonder reminds me of the constant presence of God the creator, even in the darkest nights of my life.

Even in the busyness of our days, we can develop a good habit of reflection and quiet contemplation of God's creation. If we pay attention, we can perceive God's message to us through creation.

Prayer: *Holy One, open our eyes to see the work of your hands, and open our ears to hear you through the wonder that is your creation. Amen.*

Thought for the day: God speaks to me through creation.

Julianis Báez Pichardo (Dominican Republic)

A lifelong friend

Read John 15:12–17

'I am with you always, to the end of the age.'
Matthew 28:20 (NRSV)

I never had a best friend growing up. I was a child of a career military officer, and my family moved ten times by the time I was 13 years old. It seemed that as soon as I made a friend, my father would get orders to a new duty station, sometimes thousands of miles away. I vividly remember the hugs and tears during several partings with childhood friends. When my family settled in an area for several years when I was a teenager, I had a difficult time keeping friends. I held them at arm's length, refusing to get too close emotionally. The hurt from all those childhood goodbyes truly impacted my life.

When I accepted Jesus Christ as my Saviour as an adult, I found him to be the lifelong friend I had never had. He is always with me, guiding, rescuing, helping, protecting, listening and loving me. Jesus provides all of us with everlasting joy, hope and peace. He has promised never to leave or forsake us. We can get to know Jesus by reading his words, following his example, and praising his name. Whatever life throws at us, we know we have Jesus, our friend who is just a prayer away.

Prayer: *Dear Jesus, thank you for your presence with us. Help us to stay conscious of you in all circumstances. Amen.*

Thought for the day: Jesus said, 'You are my friends if you do what I command you' (John 15:14).

Jan Willson Towne (Virginia, USA)

A light in the dark

Read Psalm 18:25–32
It is you who light my lamp; the Lord, my God, lights up my darkness.
Psalm 18:28 (NRSV)

Today's scripture takes me back to my childhood in Africa. I grew up in a poverty-stricken household among alcoholism and domestic abuse. As a result, I took refuge in books, becoming a perennial head of the class. However, as I grew older, the situation at home became heavier, leading to feelings of shame, embarrassment and low self-esteem. Bullies of all ages took advantage of this, reinforcing the ugliness I felt inside. My father, during the few times he was sober, hammered into me that a daughter was an unwelcome liability and not an asset.

However, through my mother's steadfast commitment to prayer, I learned that no hurdle was too big for God. Throughout my life, God has sent people to light my path – like my secondary-school teacher, who mentored me and painstakingly reversed all the negative beliefs I held, and my extended family, who used their resources to help and shelter me. Countless others have contributed to my life's journey.

Now that I'm a professional working with victims of domestic abuse, I realise how God used my lived experiences and hardships to prepare me for this role. When I look back now, I am more convinced than ever that God knows what is best for each one of us, and we can trust God.

Prayer: *Dear Lord, help us to put all our trust in you, especially when going through life's challenges. Amen.*

Thought for the day: People who encourage and mentor me are gifts from God.

Maureen Kambarami (England, United Kingdom)

Wise instruction

Read Proverbs 4:1–10

Then he taught me, and he said to me, 'Take hold of my words with all your heart; keep my commands, and you will live.'
Proverbs 4:4 (NIV)

When I was young, I wanted to be a skilled clarinetist. I was inspired by my grandfather who is a professional clarinetist. Though I took clarinet lessons, I regret not heeding his counsel to practise more. My grandfather attempted to lead me on the right path, but I wasn't taking his wisdom or instruction as seriously as I should have. If I had, I would have become a much more knowledgeable and skilled musician.

Similarly, our heavenly Father's words in scripture are our guide. God's instruction is a lamp to our feet, a guide to our path. God wants to lead us on good paths and to help us to become wise. When we are sensitive to and aware of the Holy Spirit's leading in our lives and the instruction God gives us, we can become wiser and more mature in our faith. Making it a priority to seek God's counsel and guidance through scripture and prayer shows our obedience to and love for God as we keep God's commandments.

Prayer: *Abba, thank you for guiding us and instructing us on the right path. Soften our hearts to be open to your instruction. In the name of the Lord Jesus Christ we pray. Amen.*

Thought for the day: Today I will seek God's counsel and wisdom in scripture.

Jordan Zuniga (California, USA)

Outer fringes

Read Job 26:7–14

These are but the outer fringe of his works; how faint the whisper we hear of him!

Job 26:14 (NIV)

Recently I was amazed at a photo of the Pillars of Creation, a star-forming region in deep space, taken by NASA's James Webb Space Telescope. It captures a breathtaking image of archlike columns of dust and gas where newly formed stars are taking shape.

Job spoke about the many unimaginable and incredible works of God. He proclaimed God's power in suspending the earth over nothing, in churning up the seas, in wrapping up the waters in the clouds, and in turning the skies fair by a simple breath. Then Job followed this with an amazing declaration: 'These are but the outer fringe of his works; how faint the whisper we hear of him!' What a thought! My mind can't fathom that the wonders of nature are just the outer fringes of God's works.

If the colours of autumn, the beauty of a first snow and the Pillars of Creation are but a faint whisper of who God is, we are indeed loved and held securely by an incomprehensible God.

Prayer: *Creator God, the concerns of this life limit our perception of who you are. Help us begin to grasp your glory that is beyond our imagining. Amen.*

Thought for the day: Every day I will listen for the whispers of God.

Valerie Bryant Bennett (Tennessee, USA)

To know God's love

Read Hosea 6:1–3

Let us acknowledge the Lord; let us press on to acknowledge him.
Hosea 6:3 (NIV)

I know my husband. I know his likes and dislikes, the food he prefers, his favourite authors. I know his way of thinking, his hopes, what saddens his heart, what makes him laugh. I know my husband because I am close to him. If I were distant and did not listen to him each day, I would not learn his preferences or worries. Even if I have the slightest doubt, I feel confident enough to approach him and ask him directly. He loves me sincerely, and I know he would follow through with an explanation to assuage my doubts.

It is the same with God. If I do not draw near to God and am not attentive to God each day, I will not recognise God's voice. I will not know what is pleasing or displeasing to God. I would question if what I am doing is acceptable; I would not know what God feels for me. But even in my uncertainty, I know I can approach God with confidence and God will answer. I can know God's will because I listen to God's word. I know of God's love because I live in the warmth of God's shelter.

Prayer: *Help us, O God, to learn more about you and draw closer to you every day. In the name of Jesus who showed us your love. Amen.*

Thought for the day: Each day is an opportunity to grow closer to God.

Dhyani Macías (Durango, Mexico)

Ancestors

I have always admired my Nana who, as a child of the Great Depression, learned not only to look for opportunities but to create them herself. When a door shut in her face, she'd pull out a crowbar and pry a dusty window open. She told me once that when she headed to college, her only intention was to get her 'MRS degree'. But by the end of her first year, she had no steady boyfriend and was failing her home-economics classes. So she pursued a psychology major and a math minor instead. When she graduated – still single – she shrugged her shoulders and figured there would be men in grad school. But it wasn't until after she'd earned a master's degree and moved across the country that she met my grandfather.

Soon they had three babies to care for, but my Nana didn't quit her work. When they moved to a new city in the 1970s, she didn't see many open opportunities for her career, so she made one for herself. She marched into her children's new school and told them why they needed a school psychologist. And then she told them why they should hire her. I grew up in that same school district, and many school counsellors told me they remembered my Nana fondly as the woman who had hired them. Her legacy is so powerful to me that it has changed the way I pursue new jobs as well. My coworkers at *The Upper Room* have reminded me of my own tenacity during the interview process. It was my Nana's persistence – which now lives in me – that got me the job.

About a year ago, as I was planning my wedding, I went shopping for a wedding dress. The moment I touched the fabric of 'the one' I began to cry. The fabric had the same texture as the eyelet curtains that had hung in my Nana's house. When I went to her nursing home to tell her all about the experience, I could tell as soon as I entered her room that something was wrong. My Nana's ever-worsening dementia meant she was no longer able to perceive my face as that of her granddaughter. She didn't recognise me anymore.

I am struck by how much I can know and feel close to a person who has little memory of me. With time, I've come to realise that I carry her memories for her. Some of them I hold in my mind, others are kept alive in letters she's written, still others live in conversations with her that I recorded when she was first diagnosed, knowing someday I would want to hear her speak lucidly again.

As my Nana's memory deteriorates, I learn more and more why people write things down, why they learn history and tradition, and why we as Christians choose to participate in a community dedicated to a book written down long ago. Even though Eve, Moses, Ruth, Isaiah, Mary and Paul all passed on long ago, their stories hold something powerful. They tell us who we are and what we are doing in this world. They connect us to God and one another so strongly that simply touching the pages of a Bible can evoke strong memories and emotions. I think this is why there are so many genealogies in the Bible. It's important that Abraham begat Isaac and Isaac begat Jacob because Isaac inherited important, life-shaping stories from his dad; Jacob inherited even more from his dad. Just as I inherited my Nana's tenacity, Matthew 1 reminds us of Jesus' heritage – a heritage that says, 'Remember David? Jesus has David's power in the face of giants. Remember Rahab? Jesus has Rahab's cunning when facing opposing authority.' Just like Jesus, we have inherited these stories as our own. We have something of each one of the characters we learn about within us, and we are called to carry on their legacy.

QUESTIONS FOR REFLECTION

1 Name a family member who has had a significant influence on you. How has that influence formed you spiritually, mentally and emotionally?

2 What character traits have you inherited from learning the stories of your biblical ancestors? What sights, sounds and textures transport you to the time when you first learned about them?

3 What legacy do you want to leave for others?

Bethany Barnett

Fully committed

Read 1 Kings 19:19–21

'Whoever wants to save their life will lose it, but whoever loses their life for me will find it.'
Matthew 16:25 (NIV)

In 2022, I used my daily devotional time to find Bible passages that I had not studied before – ones that were unmarked by my highlighter or pen. Most mornings that year I spent time in the Old Testament and gained a new appreciation for the stories and the people found there, including the call of Elisha in today's scripture reading.

When called by Elijah, Elisha slaughtered his oxen, which provided the people with a feast, a type of going-away party for Elisha. More important, it proved Elisha's commitment. To cook the meal, Elisha burned his ploughing equipment. In doing so, there was no chance of Elisha's returning to what he used to do or who he used to be. Elisha was fully committed to following and assisting Elijah.

To be faithful to God we must deny ourselves (see Luke 9:23), and in Elisha we find a beautiful example of this. Giving up old habits or turning from destructive ways can be difficult. It may mean getting help for an addiction or cutting ties with people who hinder our walk with God. Although it can be painful or uncomfortable to give up certain aspects of our lives, the closer relationship with God that we gain as a result is invaluable and incomparable.

Prayer: *Dear heavenly Father, thank you for your word and the example of faithful people like Elisha. Show us what we need to give up so that we may draw closer to you. Amen.*

Thought for the day: What do I need to give up to fully commit to God?

Julie Sipe (Pennsylvania, USA)

PRAYER FOCUS: TO FOLLOW GOD'S CALL FAITHFULLY

Hummingbird battles

Read Isaiah 65:17–25

Those who hope in the Lord will renew their strength. They will soar on wings like eagles; they will run and not grow weary, they will walk and not be faint.
Isaiah 40:31 (NIV)

Before I started watching hummingbirds, I assumed that the experience would be a calming, peaceful one. Shortly after hanging a feeder outside my window, I realised how naïve I had been! These tiny 'engines with wings' are territorial and spend much of their energy aggressively chasing and attacking any other hummingbird that dares approach. It's embarrassing to admit, but I can't help scolding them through the window: 'There's enough nectar for all of you! You don't have to fight over it! Each of you can take a spot on the feeder and all will be fed!'

But isn't that the way of the world? Across the globe, daily headlines are rife with stories of war, political scheming, oppression and intolerance. We live in a world constantly in conflict and disunion. It's easy to become weary. We long for restoration, for healing, for justice and for peace.

The good news is that in the mysterious promise of Christ's return, we will find it all. From Genesis to Revelation, scripture proclaims that our Lord will have final victory over all creation. When conflict threatens to overwhelm us, we can rest in that assurance and try to relax. What a powerful and wonderful hope we have in Jesus!

Prayer: *God of peace, when we are weighed down by the turmoil of this world, help us to remember that you have already given us perfect and lasting peace through Jesus Christ. Amen.*

Thought for the day: My hope is in the promise of Christ's new creation.

Nancy Brady-Wood (South Carolina, USA)

PRAYER FOCUS: SOMEONE WHO HAS LOST HOPE

Showing kindness

Read Luke 7:11–17
The Lord is good, a haven in a day of distress. He acknowledges those who take refuge in him.
Nahum 1:7 (CEB)

The widow in Luke 7 was in a desperate situation. She had lost her husband, and now her only son was dead. The crowd surrounding her would soon return home, and she would be alone with her grief. When Jesus saw her, he was moved. He comforted her and raised her son from the dead.

Sometimes we see people who are vulnerable, bereaved, hungry, displaced or disadvantaged. Do we pay attention or turn away? As followers of Jesus, we must not be cruel in an already cruel world. Like Christ, we must be moved by the pain of others. We are called to bring compassion and empathy to the world.

We can get stuck in our seemingly perfect worlds. It is easy to think we are more careful, more disciplined, more religious or more intelligent than those who are less fortunate. We may be tempted not to care about others' problems. But this is a narrow-minded attitude. As Christians, we can show kindness, shining the light of Christ for the world to see. We must make the world a better place by reaching out to others with compassion. The opportunity to show kindness to others is always there.

Prayer: *O Lord, help us to be compassionate to others. Guide us in showing empathy and kindness. Amen.*

Thought for the day: Today I will look for opportunities to show kindness and compassion.

Emmanuel O. Afolabi (Lagos, Nigeria)

On wings like eagles

Read Isaiah 40:26–31

Are you so foolish? After beginning by means of the Spirit, are you now trying to finish by means of the flesh?
Galatians 3:3 (NIV)

I enjoy watching the antics of the birds during the various seasons of the year. There are quite a few mentions of birds in scripture, and we know that God cares for them.

I've read that a migrating eagle flies around 98 miles per day and can reach 225 miles per day. An average eagle's wingspan is between six and seven feet. Eagles actually spend very little time in flight flapping their wings. On long flights, they usually soar on thermals until they are high enough, then they primarily glide and soar, covering a long distance without using much energy.

The Christian life is also a long, sometimes challenging journey. How do we faithfully deal with all life throws at us without growing weary and giving up? We need to learn to soar like eagles – rather than wearing ourselves out flapping our wings, we need to learn to soar in God's strength. By seeking God through scripture and prayer we can find God's 'wind' (*ruach* in Hebrew, which is also translated as 'spirit'). What good news – we can rest in God's Spirit and soar on!

Prayer: *Lord God, help us to stay near to you, so that by your Spirit we can soar in your strength. Amen.*

Thought for the day: 'Don't be afraid; you are worth more than many sparrows' (Matthew 10:31).

Ann Armstrong (England, United Kingdom)

Imitators of God

Read Colossians 3:12–17

Be imitators of God, as beloved children, and walk in love, as Christ loved us and gave himself up for us, a fragrant offering and sacrifice to God.
Ephesians 5:1–2 (NRSV)

'Socks behaves like a dog,' I was told about the resident red fox named Socks at the nature and science museum where I was a wildlife volunteer. The first day I entered his outdoor fenced-in habitat, he came running towards me wagging his fluffy orange tail. The wildlife staff explained that Socks was found and raised by a family who thought he was a puppy. By the time they realised he was a wild animal, Socks had spent too much time around humans and dogs to survive in the wild, so he was brought to the museum. Having been raised around dogs, Socks imitated the behaviour he had observed.

Christians are called to be 'imitators of God'. We are to live our lives in a way that distinguishes us from the world and not to 'imitate what is evil' (3 John 1:11). As a new believer in 1996, I learned that imitating God requires spending time with God in prayer, studying scripture and spending time with other believers who model Christian living.

Socks didn't suddenly imitate a dog, nor did I suddenly imitate God. Imitating God is an ongoing process assisted by scripture and the community of Christians.

Prayer: *Heavenly Father, thank you for your word and for other Christians who show us how to be more like you. In the name of Christ. Amen.*

Thought for the day: I imitate God when I observe, learn and apply God's word.

Debra Pierce (Massachusetts, USA)

God's instruments

Read Matthew 5:13–16

'You are the light of the world. A city on top of a hill can't be hidden.'
Matthew 5:14 (CEB)

The disturbing events in our world challenge us to reflect on our Christian calling and identity. We cannot deny the suffering and injustice around the world and in our own communities. War, gun violence and other forms of attack are ever-present. People continue to risk their lives to escape harsh conditions in the places they call home. We cannot ignore tensions among family members and friends due to our competing priorities.

All these are reflections of our broken world. And wouldn't our silence in the face of such pain be a betrayal of our calling to be God's instruments of peace, justice and healing? God has called us to let Christ's light shine where darkness prevails, and that doesn't necessarily mean that we must do something big. Our smallest acts of kindness can bring healing to a broken heart. Our honest prayers can be a source of strength for others. Our simplest acts of courage can bring justice to our communities. Let us discover the ways God is calling us to serve and intentionally strive to walk in the footsteps of Jesus.

Prayer: *Dear heavenly Father, thank you for calling us to be your servants in the world. Help us to live according to Christ's teachings. Amen.*

Thought for the day: How is God calling me to be salt and light in the world?

The Youth Group of UMC Eningen
(Baden-Württemberg, Germany)

A note of thanks

Read John 6:1–14

Jesus then took the loaves, gave thanks, and distributed to those who were seated as much as they wanted. He did the same with the fish.
John 6:11 (NIV)

My young friend had written me a thank-you note for having our neighbours over for coffee. None of the adult guests wrote, but this boy with dyslexia did. Some letters were backward, and one sentence ran on with no punctuation. He signed his name and then added the names of his two younger brothers.

I read the note with tears in my eyes. I knew how much this young man struggled with his learning disability. Yet he didn't focus on that. He focused on expressing his gratitude.

In the Bible one boy offered his five loaves and two fish to feed a multitude. Jesus took what he had and, after giving thanks, multiplied it to feed 5,000 people. That boy could have held back, telling himself that what he had was not enough; that people might laugh at him; that Jesus might reject his meagre offering; that his mother might scold him for giving away his lunch; that he would go hungry.

I keep that thank-you note to remind me to give what I have to God, trusting that God's power can make it enough.

Prayer: *Dear God, help us to remember to look to you in faith and give what we have, knowing you will multiply our gifts for the good of the world. In Jesus' name. Amen.*

Thought for the day: In the hands of God, my gifts are made sufficient.

Zoe M. Hicks (Georgia, USA)

Faithful and just

Read Psalm 32:1–5

The one the Lord doesn't consider guilty – in whose spirit there is no dishonesty – that one is truly happy!
Psalm 32:2 (CEB)

I have played the piano for over 20 years in a variety of settings, and now I am blessed to be a church pianist and a piano teacher. Playing through a song without making any mistakes is a goal that even the most talented pianists can only hope to achieve. My years of learning and practising have helped me to make fewer mistakes, and the ones I do make often go unnoticed by those listening. But I am aware of every wrong note I play. I have to be willing to forgive myself for them while pushing myself to try harder next time.

Similarly, God knows about the mistakes we make in our daily lives, including the sins that no one knows about. These mistakes can't be undone, but they can always be confessed to God – who is 'faithful and just to forgive' (1 John 1:9). As someone who is guilty of worse things than playing the wrong notes, I feel grateful when I remember that God sees every wrong I commit but is still willing to forgive me. God always gives me another chance to do things better. This continual forgiveness is the attitude I wish to have and to inspire in others.

Prayer: *Thank you, Lord, for forgiving our sins and giving us a chance to live free from guilt. Help us to show forgiveness to others. In Jesus' name. Amen.*

Thought for the day: When I confess my sins, God is faithful and just to forgive them.

James Cain (Kentucky, USA)

A special bond

Read Ephesians 4:1–6

Encourage one another and build each other up, just as in fact you are doing.
1 Thessalonians 5:11 (NIV)

When I was sick with pneumonia six years ago, my daughter-in-law Carol became my caregiver. She is a medical doctor and decided to take time off to care for me in the hospital and later at home. Recently I had cataract surgery, and again she nursed me back to health. Not only does Carol have the knowledge and skill as a doctor, but she also has an incredible amount of patience. Above all, she is a woman of deep faith. Our love for each other and our faith in Jesus Christ strengthens our bond even more.

This reminds me of the beautiful relationship between Ruth and Naomi in the Bible. Naomi's steadfast faith and love for God and Ruth's commitment to Naomi brought them closer together. Through tragedy, they held on to faith and each other as they made their way back to Judah for a fresh start (see Ruth 1).

Relationships within families are special and complex. While they can bring much joy, they can also bring challenges. Our faith can be a powerful source of sustenance during trying times. Our relationships and love for God can help us to navigate challenges and to cherish moments of joy.

Prayer: *Creator God, thank you for sustaining us and protecting us. Fill us with your unfailing grace and abiding presence. In Jesus' name. Amen.*

Thought for the day: Relationships are a gift from God.

Navamani Peter (Karnataka, India)

Our daily bread

Read Matthew 14:13–19

He gave thanks and broke the loaves.
Matthew 14:19 (NIV)

It was early morning as I quietly worked in the kitchen, carefully measuring and weighing the yeast, the flour, the sugar and a pinch of salt. As I mixed the ingredients, the Lord's Prayer came to mind: 'Give us this day our daily bread.' After mixing the dough, I left it in a warm place to rise, then sat for a while and thought of how often I've rambled through the Lord's Prayer without giving much thought to the words.

Later, as I kneaded and formed the dough, I recalled how Jesus broke bread, lifted it heavenward and gave thanks to God. I couldn't help but wonder what Jesus was thankful for. Was he thankful for the farmer who planted the tiny grain of wheat? For the sun that warmed the earth, enabling the wheat to grow? Was he thankful for the gentle rain that brought life to that tiny grain of wheat?

Later, as the aroma of freshly baked bread filled the kitchen, I thought of how Jesus must have been thankful for the miracle of nature – for the sun and the rain and everything that went into making a simple loaf of bread. We too can remember those whose hands helped to make the bread we eat, raising our eyes heavenward to give thanks to God.

Prayer: *O God, how often we take for granted the bounty of your goodness! Help us remember that the food on our table is given by you and that without you and your love, we would have nothing. Amen.*

Thought for the day: I can see the hand of the creator in all things.

Iris Alderson (Massachusetts, USA)

Always listening

Read Philippians 4:4–9

Rejoice always, pray continually, give thanks in all circumstances; for this is God's will for you in Christ Jesus.
1 Thessalonians 5:16–18 (NIV)

One evening I was sitting on the church steps with my pastor before a committee meeting. We were chatting when suddenly my pastor exclaimed, 'Oh, I haven't prayed today!' This abrupt confession surprised me; I did not understand prayer that way. But my pastor's frankness highlighted the significance of prayer and inspired me to communicate more frequently and informally with God.

Many years have passed since that experience. I have grown in my faith, and my journey continues. Now my conversations with God are frequent and serene. When I awake in the morning, I express my gratitude for a night's rest and the new opportunities awaiting me. During my day, I give thanks for both rewarding and challenging encounters. As my day winds down, I can think of my blessings and rest peacefully. And throughout the day, God is there awaiting our moments together.

As Christians, we are greatly blessed to worship a God who is eager to hear from and commune with us. We are encouraged to share our thoughts, admissions, supplications, desires and praise! God awaits our prayers.

Prayer: *Thank you, ever-listening God, for being ready and eager to hear our thoughts and prayers. Amen.*

Thought for the day: God is always eager to hear from me.

John Alter (Florida, USA)

Giving from the heart

Read Luke 21:1–4

'All these people gave their gifts out of their wealth; but she out of her poverty put in all she had to live on.'
Luke 21:4 (NIV)

I observed that some religious education classes at my church needed a guitarist. Without music, the children were less enthusiastic in praising the Lord. I was not gifted in music, but my heart longed to serve God. So I asked my brother who played guitar to teach me. Though I could not master the instrument, my presence as a guitarist helped the children to sing more joyfully to God; my heart was joyful as well.

What I experienced reminds me of the poor widow who found favour in God's eyes though she offered only two small coins. Perhaps what we give is nothing in the eyes of people, but our willingness makes God glad. Then joy and peace shall fill our hearts. Our lives will be blessed as we put God above all matters.

We do not need to be perfect in order to serve God. So whenever the Spirit moves us to share our talent or to give what we have for God's work in the world, we can freely offer it to God. Our longing to please God is what is most important.

Prayer: *Dear God, we often doubt the value of what we have to give. Help us to realise that you pay attention to the sincerity of our hearts more than to the gifts themselves. Amen.*

Thought for the day: I will not hesitate to offer what I have to the Lord.

Kumalawaty Sundari (Jakarta, Indonesia)

Never forgotten

Read Isaiah 49:14–18

'Behold, I have graven thee upon the palms of my hands; thy walls are continually before me.'
Isaiah 49:16 (KJV)

No matter their age, children who have been abandoned by a parent may struggle with feeling unloved. They may wonder how the person who should love them the most could leave them. As a child of divorce, raised by a single parent, I often wondered this myself. Even though I had one parent who loved me unconditionally and cared for me, I questioned why the other did not. Feelings of loneliness and unworthiness filled me. I felt alone in my sadness.

But today's scripture from Isaiah changed my perspective and my life. It showed me that I was not the only person to harbour these feelings. And it reminded me that God will never forget me. I am written on the palms of God's hands! This truth brings me peace beyond words.

Now I choose to be thankful for God's unfailing love and for the people in my life who truly care about me. Life can be unfair; but when we recognise that God's love for us is real and never-ending, our lives are changed in unimaginable ways. God is so good!

Prayer: *Dear Lord, thank you for your love and for your promise never to leave us. Thank you for the people you have placed in our lives who show us your love. Amen.*

Thought for the day: I can find peace knowing that God loves me always.

Jaime Ginn (Alabama, USA)

Praying first

Read 1 John 5:13–15

Jesus told his disciples a parable to show them that they should always pray and not give up.
Luke 18:1 (NIV)

I have played golf for many years, but my skills needed improvement; so I decided to take a lesson. The professional who worked with me was very helpful and pointed out several things I could do to improve. I had previously tried many other methods, but they hadn't worked. It turned out that seeking professional guidance was the right solution.

Whether it is a challenge with work, family or friends, I often try to solve the issue on my own. Sometimes I am fortunate enough to figure things out. But many times it's only after multiple options have failed that I finally pray about the situation and seek guidance from God. When I reflect on this pattern of behaviour, it doesn't make any sense. Prayer should be the steering wheel that guides our life, not the spare tyre we pull out in emergencies.

When we face challenges in life, our first step should be to go to God in prayer. Our heavenly Father created us and knows us better than we know ourselves. God will not only provide the guidance we need but will give us peace as well.

Prayer: *Dear heavenly Father, it is a great privilege to come to you in prayer. Help us to seek your guidance in all matters, big and small. Amen.*

Thought for the day: Prayer is my first option, not a last resort.

John D. Bown (Minnesota, USA)

Love and trust

Read 1 Samuel 1:12–28

'I prayed for this child, and the Lord has granted me what I asked of him. So now I give him to the Lord. For his whole life he shall be given over to the Lord.'
1 Samuel 1:27–28 (NIV)

Shortly after I was born, my mother became ill and was prescribed a potent medication that severely impaired her ability to focus. But that didn't stop her from sharing Christ with me. And she always encouraged me in my studies and cheered me on in sports, even while dealing with her pain and debilitating condition. She always reached out to me physically and emotionally. When it was time for me to leave home, it was very difficult for Mum; but she trusted that God would guide me in the way I should go.

Hannah is a great example of this kind of love and trust. After she cried out to the Lord, God blessed her with a baby boy, Samuel. And Hannah kept her commitment to devote her son to God. Though she loved Samuel, she was willing to step aside and let him grow with God. Hannah showed her devoted and sacrificial love both in her desire to have a child and in her willingness to give the child to the Lord's work. Hannah's love is an example of what it looks like to support and also let go. It's not easy letting go; but if we trust and have faith in the Lord, all will be well.

Prayer: *Faithful God, help us to support those we love in their service to you. Amen.*

Thought for the day: I can entrust those I love to God.

Masego Mohlanga (Gauteng, South Africa)

A closer look

Read Isaiah 43:19–23

See, I am doing a new thing! Now it springs up; do you not perceive it?
I am making a way in the wilderness and streams in the wasteland.
Isaiah 43:19 (NIV)

I followed signs to a sunflower field, expecting to see a multitude of flowers in full bloom. But what I found was a huge collection of dead and blackened stumps.

Though at first put off by the starkness of the place, I stood still and studied the scene. I heard many bird sounds and saw a wren darting in and out of the stalks, searching for seeds. A couple of little yellow birds – goldfinches perhaps – darted past me. Other birds I could not identify were also there along with several monarch butterflies fluttering about. And I saw several wild, blue morning glories winding up the dead stalks of the sunflowers. The site that seemed dead at first glance was teeming with life.

The words of Isaiah came to mind: 'I am doing a new thing… Do you not perceive it?' God is working in places that may seem dry and dead. We may look around us and not immediately see any signs of new life. Yet when we take a closer look, life surprises us. God's creative power will never disappoint.

Prayer: *Creator and Sustainer, thank you for your ongoing creative power that brings new life to the world. Amen.*

Thought for the day: God's creative power is at work – even when I can't immediately see it.

Mike C. Bertoglio (Georgia, USA)

Walking prayers

Read Galatians 6:7–10

Let us not become weary in doing good, for at the proper time we will reap a harvest if we do not give up.
Galatians 6:9 (NIV)

Our church has organised a walking prayer ministry. We use a little treasure chest for our prayer requests. Gathering at the local high school track, people write their requests on a card and then place it in the chest. As prayer walkers arrive, they pick out a card and take off walking, praying for the request on the card. Sometimes they keep the same card the entire time they walk, and sometimes they change cards with each lap around the track.

When we began this practice, I was inspired by one elderly woman who walked each week. I hoped that when I reached her age, I would still be setting a faithful example of prayer for others.

While I walk and pray, my young grandchildren play on the field inside the track. One day my grandson picked up a pen and a card. His sister scolded him, 'You can only write notes to God on those cards.' I later found notes in the treasure chest written in her childish scribble: 'I love God.' 'God is nice.' Then I realised that my grandchildren were learning some important lessons too – that prayer is one way we exercise our faith just as we exercise our body.

Prayer: *Father God, help us to know that our actions can lead someone to you. Amen.*

Thought for the day: My faithful actions can encourage others.

Joni Topper (Texas, USA)

Inner being

Read Ephesians 3:14–21
I pray that out of his glorious riches he may strengthen you with power through his Spirit in your inner being.
Ephesians 3:16 (NIV)

It is important to take care of our inner being. I know that if I don't take care of my mental health properly, I will suffer.

One afternoon, I went for a walk. I saw that my neighbour was cleaning his car. He was meticulous and careful, cleaning every little part.

As I watched him, I was reminded of how important it is to clean our minds and hearts every day. What is weighing us down? What do we need to give to God? I am a better Christian, sister, wife, friend, mentor and servant when I spend time with God examining my inner world.

God wants to strengthen our inner being. God will always help us to renew our hearts and minds so we can shine from the inside out.

Prayer: *Dear God, help us grow spiritually healthier as you strengthen our inner being. As Jesus taught us, we pray, 'Father, hallowed be your name, your kingdom come. Give us each day our daily bread. Forgive us our sins, for we also forgive everyone who sins against us. And lead us not into temptation' (Luke 11:2–4). Amen.*

Thought for the day: Today I will take time to examine my heart.

Mateja Stolnik Vugrek (Zagreb, Croatia)

Your will be done

Read Galatians 5:22–26
'Be still, and know that I am God!'
Psalm 46:10 (NRSV)

I am currently halfway through a 20-year prison sentence for thefts I committed while addicted to drugs and alcohol. As the years have slowly passed, I have spent more than a few sleepless nights thinking and believing that my whole life is just one big mistake. How could God possibly love me or use me in this cold, lonely prison environment?

But lately I have come to see that God has been preparing me for greater things. About a year ago, the prison hired me to be a peer mentor. I now get the opportunity to practise the spiritual fruits of love, patience, kindness and generosity that I have developed after years of being confined to prison with ample time to 'be still'.

Recently, I was promoted to a Peer Recovery Specialist. As such, I will be able to use my life experiences with substance abuse and mental illness to help other men who are struggling with the same issues. Just when I was ready to give up, God showed up and made God's will for my life crystal clear. My life in prison now has purpose. Each day I am able to help someone society has cast aside.

Prayer: *Almighty God, help us to reach out to your children and lift them up from their despair. Amen.*

Thought for the day: God works in mysterious ways; I will be ready when God calls.

Christopher King (Virginia, USA)

Embracing the unexpected

Read Job 5:8–16

Do not boast about tomorrow, for you do not know what a day may bring.
Proverbs 27:1 (NIV)

When I first started leading the children's message at my church, it felt like an obligation and made me a little nervous. But I have found a formula that works well for me. First I think of something important or interesting that happened during the week. Then I relate the experience to a child's or teenager's perspective, and I choose a Bible verse to support the lesson. I now look forward to the weekly ritual of transforming an ordinary moment from my life into a shared experience of God. These messages are not just for the children; I believe they are God's messages to me personally.

I remember working on a particular message in which I reflected on a week my family had experienced that was full of good and bad surprises. I planned to talk about how God is always with us in times of trial, but the message God revealed to me was that unexpected situations offer us opportunities to celebrate with or to support one another. Surprises jolt us out of our routines so that we can be God's hands and feet in the world, offering and receiving praise and support.

Now I relish the time I spend with God each week to prepare a message for the children, and I take great comfort and joy in each surprise that God brings my way.

Prayer: *Dear God, when we experience the unexpected, help us to be at peace, trusting in your grace and blessings for us. Amen.*

Thought for the day: Today I will embrace God's message for me in the unexpected.

Melissa Dameron-Vines (Alabama, USA)

God's timing

Read Psalm 40:1–13

I am poor and needy; may the Lord think of me. You are my help and my deliverer; you are my God, do not delay.
Psalm 40:17 (NIV)

I had to travel about two hours from my home to the city of Bayamón, Puerto Rico, for a work meeting, so I took public transport. In the morning I rode a passenger van to Bayamón. Later that day, I went to the public transport counter to arrange my trip home. The agent told me that the only van available would take me as far as Santa Isabel but not to my town. I decided to take it, and we arrived in Santa Isabel late. The last van there had left for the evening, and no other option was available.

As I stood outside the public transport office, I said aloud: 'Please, Lord Jesus, send one of your angels to help me.' Ten minutes later a transport van pulled up, and the driver asked where I was going. When I told him, he replied: 'Get in; that's where I'm headed.' As we got underway he told me he wasn't sure why he came that way, and I told him God nudged him in this direction because I had been praying for God's help. With a grateful heart, I recalled the words of the psalmist: 'I waited patiently for the Lord; he turned to me and heard my cry' (Psalm 40:1).

Prayer: *Loving God, thank you for hearing our cries. When we are most in need, you are always there beside us. Amen.*

Thought for the day: God is my ever-present help in trouble (see Psalm 46:1).

Víctor Lugo Pérez (Puerto Rico)

PRAYER FOCUS: PUBLIC TRANSPORT DRIVERS

The master's voice

Read John 10:1–10

'When he has brought out all his own, he goes on ahead of them, and his sheep follow him because they know his voice.'
John 10:4 (NIV)

Recently I've spent a lot of time counting sheep. This is not to try to sooth myself to sleep; it's because a group of intrepid sheep have decided that my lawn is much tastier than the grass in their own field. After several attempts at sending them back, I usually give up and phone the farmer, our neighbour Lynda.

One day when she arrived, Lynda took one look at the flock and shouted, 'Come here!' I watched in amazement as the sheep turned round and, bleating loudly, surged forward, running down our garden to meet her.

My thoughts instantly flew to Jesus' words, 'His sheep follow him because they know his voice.' Witnessing those sheep's immediate recognition to Lynda's voice brought the whole parable to life for me – it was almost being enacted before my eyes. Yes, I'd read that verse many times before, but suddenly those words had a much greater impact upon me.

I learnt a lesson I shall never forget that day – to engage more deeply and imaginatively with the words of the Bible and to focus on them with all my mind, heart and soul.

Prayer: *Dear Lord, thank you for all the ways that you speak to us, even in the everyday happenings of life. Amen.*

Thought for the day: 'The word of God is alive and active' (Hebrews 4:12).

D. Carole Wilsher (Wales, United Kingdom)

The words to pray

Read Romans 8:26–30

The Spirit helps us in our weakness, for we do not know how to pray as we ought, but that very Spirit intercedes with groanings too deep for words.

Romans 8:26 (NRSV)

My mum and dad taught me at a very early age to pray. But I struggle from time to time with how and what to pray. Our family regularly attended church and prayer services, and at times we prayed at the church altar if we felt led to do so. But sometimes even now I'm not sure what to say when I pray.

Memorised prayers and scriptures help when I'm stumbling over my thoughts while trying to verbalise them in prayer. My dad's favourite scripture is Proverbs 3:5–6, which begins, 'Trust in the Lord with all thine heart' (KJV). These verses keep my mind focused when I wake up worried or run into any problem. They remind me how trustworthy our heavenly Father is. Mum's favourite scripture is Proverbs 17:22, 'A merry heart doeth good like a medicine' (KJV). What great reminders of the Father's desire to lead us to joy, peace and healing!

Sometimes I still don't know what to pray, and I get stuck. I told Mum my dilemma years ago, and her simple answer was: 'Just pray his name: Jesus, Jesus, Jesus.' Praying that beautiful, sweet name has saved my life. There is amazing power in Jesus' name.

Prayer: *Jesus, Jesus, Jesus. Amen.*

Thought for the day: Scripture guides me when I don't know what to pray.

Matthew B. Harper (West Virginia, USA)

God will provide

Read Matthew 6:25–34

'Your Father knows what you need before you ask him.'
Matthew 6:8 (NIV)

In 2023, my family and I had to move out of the house we had been renting. The owner told us that he would be renovating it, so we needed to find another place to live. We prepared for the moving costs several months in advance. Later my sister learned of an additional cost – 200,000 Indonesian rupiahs, just over 12 US dollars – which we had not prepared for. She did not tell me about it at first but decided to wait and tell me later.

The next morning I sent a message to a friend to let her know we would soon be moving. She responded and said that she wanted to send me some money for our moving needs, which she did. I told my sister about the money, and she became very excited. That was when she mentioned the additional cost, which the friend's money slightly exceeded. We decided to give the small amount of money that remained back to God as an offering of thanks.

In today's quoted scripture, Jesus says that God knows what we need even before we ask. In my experience, God not only knew my need but filled it before I even knew to ask! This is why Jesus says in Matthew 6 not to worry. From then on, I decided not to be anxious about my needs because God cares for me.

Prayer: *Merciful God, help us to trust that you know our needs and will care for us. Amen.*

Thought for the day: God knows my needs and will provide.

Linawati Santoso (East Java, Indonesia)

Seeing the light

Read John 8:12–20
'I am the light of the world. Whoever follows me will never walk in darkness, but will have the light of life.'
John 8:12 (NIV)

My sister and I enjoyed a lovely walk in the early evening, in order to have a meal in a restaurant with some of our church family. When we were going home some hours later, what a difference there was in the journey! It was now dark, so the path was much more difficult to follow, and the absence of street lights made the walk seem even longer. We soon linked arms to keep in step and go in the same direction until eventually the lights from the train station were visible in the distance, which made it easier to see our destination.

It was only later that I remembered I had a small torch in my handbag all along. This would have given us immediate light on the path ahead and made our walk back much easier and safer, had I used it. In the same way, how often do we struggle along in our own strength – or even with the assistance of other Christians – but forget to lean on Christ, our light?

When we make Jesus our first helper, the situation changes for the better!

Prayer: *Dear God, we pray for those who are going through dark times just now, that the light of Christ may guide their steps and that they will have helpful companions on the road. Amen.*

Thought for the day: Jesus is always ready to help me.

Christine Hay (Scotland, United Kingdom)

Never forgotten

Read Psalm 139:13–18

Can a woman forget her nursing child or show no compassion for the child of her womb? Even these might forget, yet I will not forget you.
Isaiah 49:15 (NRSV)

After more than 60 years of marriage, my father could no longer care for my mother at home. Her advancing Alzheimer's disease required her to move into the memory-care unit at a skilled nursing facility. My wife and I drove several hours for our first visit in Mum's new room.

My mother knew who we were but struggled to talk. Her thoughts became tangled, getting lost between her mind and her mouth. I hugged Mum while tears of frustration wet her cheeks. But she perked up when we pushed her wheelchair around the fenced-in patio to see the flowers.

When we said goodbye, Mum had a clear moment. She clasped my hands in hers, looked deep into my eyes, and said, 'I love you. The next time you come, I may not remember who you are. But remember that I love you – always.' Her declaration of love reminded me of God's promise in today's reading. Though illness or injury may steal our memories, God will never forget us.

Prayer: *Faithful God, help us be patient with those whose minds are failing. Thank you for assuring us that your love and care are everlasting. Amen.*

Thought for the day: God will always remember me.

David Brannock (Tennessee, USA)

Justice and mercy

Read Matthew 20:1–16

'But he answered one of them, "I am not being unfair to you, friend. Didn't you agree to work for a denarius? Take your pay and go. I want to give the one who was hired last the same as I gave you."'
Matthew 20:13–14 (NIV)

One day my grandfather told me we were going to our family's land to pick 'ground apples'. We picked up thousands of fist-sized rocks and threw them into the back of a pickup truck. It was hot, dusty, exhausting work. The next time my grandfather suggested we pick ground apples, I suggested maybe I should get paid for it. From then on, I was paid an hourly rate for every job I did. Fair is fair.

Then I read today's scripture story in Matthew 20, and I found it confusing and unfair. I thought the people who worked all day should have been paid a lot more than the people who only worked one hour. But in time I realised that this story is about justice for the all-day workers and mercy for the part-day workers. The all-day workers got paid what they had agreed to. Perhaps the part-day workers with a lower wage would have been distressed and unable to afford food.

I now understand that justice and mercy are two sides of one coin, and that coin is God's love. Micah 6:8 says it best: 'What does the Lord require of you? To act justly and to love mercy and to walk humbly with your God.'

Prayer: *Loving God, may we remember that justice and mercy go hand-in-hand and that one without the other creates imbalance. Amen.*

Thought for the day: Today I will treat others with justice and mercy.

Trudy Rankin (Victoria, Australia)

Into the deep

Read Luke 5:1–11

'Put out into the deep water and let down your nets for a catch.'
Luke 5:4 (NRSV)

When I was growing up, in the summer we often had a beach hut. A highlight was the visit of my grandparents. Grandad would be in his Sunday best suit complete with trilby hat and a flower in his buttonhole.

Then came the great adventure. He would roll up his trousers to the knee and then roll up his long johns. Barefoot, hand in hand, we would paddle just along the water's edge. But, cautious as ever, if the water lapped up over his ankles, quick as a flash my grandfather would be out of the water, safe on the beach. He did not want to run the risk of being dragged out into the deeper water.

But that is just what God wants for us. When Jesus told the disciples to 'put out into the deep water', they caught so many fish they had to call for help to haul in the nets. In the same way, Jesus doesn't want us to stay forever in the 'spiritual shallows'. He wants us to venture out into even deeper spiritual waters with him. Yet, all too often, like my beloved grandfather, we feel safer in the shallows.

Prayer: *Dear Lord, give us the courage to step out boldly into the deeper waters of our faith and experience, knowing that you seek to deepen our understanding of you and your love for each one of us. Amen.*

Thought for the day: When I venture into deeper 'water' with God, amazing and surprising things can and will happen.

Peter Edwards (England, United Kingdom)

Get up again!

Read Proverbs 24:10–16

Though the righteous fall seven times, they rise again, but the wicked stumble when calamity strikes.
Proverbs 24:16 (NIV)

I had undergone major surgery and was hospitalised for three weeks when we suddenly lost our source of income. We were forced to sell our house in order to avoid being crushed by the mortgage. An inner voice nagged me: *You are not a good enough Christian; God would have prevented this. You should have prayed with more faith. This is the end.* All I could say in prayer was, 'Help!'

I then remembered today's verse from Proverbs and found solace. Knowing that even godly people can fall took away my sense of guilt. It also gave me hope that I would get up again – no matter how severe my circumstances were.

Proverbs 24:16 rang true when I reflected on the many hardships my husband and I had already overcome. God lifted us each time. This encouraged me to get up and get on with life, knowing we would overcome this new setback as well.

God didn't promise a smooth life without obstacles, setbacks or challenges. Yet, as God's children, we have a privileged position: God is by our side throughout the journey – no matter what. We must not let obstacles define us or keep us down. With God on our side, we will get up again.

Prayer: *Dear Lord, help us to see your faithfulness in every situation. Thank you for helping us get up when we fall. Amen.*

Thought for the day: When I fall, God will help me get up again.

Christel Owoo (Greater Accra Region, Ghana)

An abundant catch

Read Matthew 4:18–22

'I was hungry and you gave me food to eat. I was thirsty and you gave me a drink. I was a stranger and you welcomed me.'
Matthew 25:35 (CEB)

Years ago I lived in Key West, Florida. One morning we were catching mahi-mahi almost as fast as we could bait the hooks. We realised we had more fish than we could eat, so we headed back to shore. The skipper gave us an address where we could take the extra fish.

Six nights a week, the Catholic Sisters served supper to people living in poverty. We gave them our fish and were invited back for dinner. As the Mother Superior blessed the meal, she said, 'A Catholic, a Protestant and a Jew provided our meal tonight. Regardless of your heritage, all are welcome to eat at God's table.'

Our gift was simple – indeed the fish would have spoiled if we hadn't given them away. However, it transformed the rest of my time in Key West. Hardly a week went by when someone didn't stop me on the street and ask, 'Aren't you the guy who brought us the fish? God bless you.'

Until then I had never seen those people who were struggling. People are still struggling. Look around at those who are cold, lonely and hungry. There are countless ways to support them. The rewards of giving far exceed the value of the gift.

Prayer: *Dear God, thank you for opportunities to share what we have. Open our eyes to the people in need around us and guide us to support them. Amen.*

Thought for the day: God can do great things with simple gifts.

Raymond Ross (Colorado, USA)

From sadness to joy

Read Zephaniah 3:9–17

When I said, 'My foot is slipping,' your unfailing love, Lord, supported me. When anxiety was great within me, your consolation brought me joy.
Psalm 94:18–19 (NIV)

For several days I had been suffering from joint and lower-back pain. I was constantly grumbling and talking about my physical pain, and I was weighed down with an attitude of defeat.

I didn't realise how my behaviour was affecting my state of mind and relationship with my family, but my daughters noticed it because I wasn't laughing at their banter or interacting with them in their conversations. I remained serious, expressing no emotion. My oldest daughter asked me, 'Mum, why don't you laugh?' Several responses ran through my mind. The first ones were all the valid excuses I had related to my physical pain. But then came a gentle persuasion from God encouraging me to change my attitude.

The Holy Spirit has graced us with the gift of joy. Instead of focusing on my pain, weakness and exhaustion, I could choose to lean into the unwavering joy of God. When I began to laugh again with my children, my spirit was lighter and my attitude was transformed.

We can live joyfully, even in the throes of pain. God can bring us the fulfilment of such joy when we align ourselves with God's will.

Prayer: *Loving God, even in our pain help us experience your joy and love. Lord, in your mercy, hear our prayer. Amen.*

Thought for the day: God fills my soul with joy.

Tamie L. Ruperto (Virginia, USA)

God walks with us

Read Isaiah 41:8–16

I the Lord thy God will hold thy right hand, saying unto thee, Fear not;
I will help thee.
Isaiah 41:13 (KJV)

While driving home one day, I stopped at a pedestrian crosswalk to let a young girl and her father cross the road. They held hands as she happily skipped along. She was carefree, eagerly looking up at her dad and talking to him. She never looked where she was stepping or paid any attention to the cars on either side of the crosswalk.

At home, I considered how my walk with the Lord is meant to reflect what I had witnessed. Did I trust my heavenly Father to hold my hand and get me safely through life's challenges? I could think of several times in my life where I had taken matters into my own hands, impatient and refusing to trust the process to God.

When we try to work things out on our own, the 'what ifs' and 'maybes' keep us in a place of anxiety and stress. But as we read in scripture, 'I the Lord thy God will hold thy right hand, saying unto thee, Fear not; I will help thee.' Just as the little girl trusted her father, we can trust our heavenly Father to walk beside us and keep us safe.

Prayer: *Faithful Lord, help us to trust your promise never to leave us, nor forsake us. Lead us beside still and quiet waters as we keep our focus on you. Amen.*

Thought for the day: God walks beside me every moment of the day.

Sohani Faria (British Columbia, Canada)

A good time to pray

Read James 5:13–16

'Where two or three are gathered in my name, I'm there with them.'
Matthew 18:20 (CEB)

The cancer centre waiting room where I sat was crowded with patients and caregivers. A woman came in pushing a young person in a wheelchair who looked to be her daughter. The woman took the seat next to me and parked the wheelchair immediately in front of me. My first thought was, *How rude! I can't even move my feet or get up.* But I bit my tongue and said nothing.

Shortly thereafter, I noticed the young woman had pulled out a daily devotional and was reading an article entitled 'Get close to God.' This inspired me to pull out my phone and begin reading my daily devotionals too. My first one centred on Matthew 18:20 and the second, James 5:13.

My mood changed as I looked around the room and thought, *Who in this room filled with patients and caregivers is not suffering?* As I began to pray silently, I wondered how many others were using this time to pray. I could feel God's presence with us and knew that God was hearing our prayers. God will gladly join us in our prayers at any time and any place.

Prayer: *Heavenly Father, help us to take the time to pray and rest in the assurance that you are listening. Amen.*

Thought for the day: I can use times of waiting to connect with God.

Gregory Shanley (Michigan, USA)

God's embrace

Read Psalm 56

You yourself have kept track of my misery. Put my tears into your bottle – aren't they on your scroll already?
Psalm 56:8 (CEB)

I volunteer at a women's prison. One of the highlights of my year is the annual Christmas gathering. Inmates and volunteers all pack into a huge gym, sitting side by side as guest speakers and worship leaders share messages of hope and encouragement. We enjoy two hours of worship and prayer, clapping and singing. The gathering concludes with volunteers distributing care packages to each inmate.

This year something different and life-changing happened. The chaplain asked the volunteers to come to the front of the room. She said to the inmates, 'These women are here to pray with you; if you want prayer, come forward.' Every woman in the gym stood up! We watched silently as, one by one, women stepped forward to receive prayer, bravely sharing their pain and heartache. A few times, I felt a woman rest her head on my shoulder, like a child with her mother. More than once, I noticed teardrops landing on my shoes during the prayer.

These images reminded me of how God pays attention to our every tear and embraces us in our sorrow. As I thought about this, I truly experienced what it means to be the hands and feet of Christ.

Prayer: *Dear God, thank you for comforting us like a mother comforts her child. Help us to turn to you in difficult times and to be a place of safety and refuge for others. Amen.*

Thought for the day: Like a loving mother, God holds us close.

Angie Gage (South Carolina, USA)

Trust the driver

Read Isaiah 41:8–10

*'My thoughts are not your thoughts, neither are your ways my ways,'
declares the Lord.*
Isaiah 55:8 (NIV)

I've always loved the English language, but I never considered that passion to be a viable career. I told myself that I needed to finish a degree and find a corporate job after graduation to feel like a responsible adult. I studied business administration out of desperation. Now I can see how God had been preparing me all along. In my university days, I served as a translator for my Chinese friend, and now I work as an English teacher. It has been 10 years since I started working as an English teacher, and I'm able to provide for myself and help my family. The work of God continuously astounds me.

Sometimes our lack of imagination and our desire for control limit what we think we can do and achieve. When we try to become the driver of our lives, we forget that it is God who leads the way.

God can guide us down roads we have never seen or imagined. While we see only what's right in front of us, God sees the entire journey. Let us surrender our lives to God's guidance.

Prayer: *Heavenly Father, thank you for your patience and love for us. May we share your love with the people around us. Amen.*

Thought for the day: When my view is limited, I can trust God to guide the way.

Jether Ann Rizaldo (Cordillera Administrative Region, Philippines)

True hospitality

Read Hebrews 13:1–2

Do not neglect to show hospitality to strangers, for by doing that some have entertained angels without knowing it.
Hebrews 13:2 (NRSV)

When I was young I overhead someone say that I could not sing. I have carried a sense of shame about this all my life. Following a move, I decided to try to lay this 'ghost' to rest. I plucked up the courage and went to a community choir. No one spoke to me the whole evening, except to show me where to pay. I did not know where to sit, what to do or what I needed to have. I left at the interval very disheartened and wondered if I would have the courage to try again.

Thankfully I did. Two weeks later I tried a new choir. As I got out of the car, I was noticed and welcomed. Several people spoke to me and offered me help. They invited me to sit with them and showed me what we were doing. They introduced me to others. They expressed the hope that I would come back. No one mentioned money!

Now, I know I am no angel, but I felt very cared for and very grateful. Those present showed me true hospitality without condition. While, as with a life of faith, there does come a time for commitment, there was no pressure on me. They accepted me as I was. In doing so they reflected for me the true hospitality of God: loving, welcoming, unconditional. I felt like an honoured guest.

Prayer: *Lord, thank you for your generous hospitality to us. We pray that we offer the same gift to those who come to us as guests.*

Thought for the day: True hospitality has the power to change lives.

Jane Haslam (England, United Kingdom)

Live your life

Read Deuteronomy 31:1–8

'The Lord himself goes before you and will be with you; he will never leave you nor forsake you. Do not be afraid; do not be discouraged.'
Deuteronomy 31:8 (NIV)

In 2019, I was in eighth grade and new to my school. I felt like I had no one. I was always quiet and alone, even during lunch breaks.

One Friday, I went to school wearing a dress that looked old – like it was my grandmother's. But it wasn't. I wore it because all my clothes were in bad shape, and that dress seemed like the best option I had. But when I entered the classroom, my classmates burst out laughing. I had to fight back tears, but I knew God was with me. I prayed silently for strength and power, and I stood up and told them to go ahead and laugh but that I felt good in the dress. I even twirled around to show them how confident I was in it.

I have realised that this is my life, which I was given by God. I should do things that make me happy and stop doing things that don't make me happy just to please other people. I'm fine with God alone!

Prayer: *Dear God, give us light. When we fall, lift us up. When we lose our way, be our guide. Amen.*

Thought for the day: I can be confident with God by my side.

Lethabo Molotjwa (Gauteng, South Africa)

A change in perspective

Read Isaiah 55:8–11

Trust in the Lord with all your heart and lean not on your own understanding.
Proverbs 3:5 (NIV)

I was working on a puzzle with my three-year-old granddaughter. It was from a set of puzzles of different shapes and sizes. This one had only eight pieces. Four of the pieces went together easily, but we couldn't make the others work. I finally said, 'Summer, we must be missing a piece, or these pieces are from a different puzzle.' And I gave up.

But after a minute, Summer said, 'Grandma, I got these two pieces to fit.' And she had! It turns out that we had been looking at the puzzle from the wrong perspective; changing our perspective enabled us to finish the puzzle easily.

In today's scripture reading from Isaiah, the Lord says, 'As the heavens are higher than the earth, so are my ways higher than your ways and my thoughts than your thoughts' (v. 9). And Proverbs encourages us to 'trust in the Lord with all [our] heart and lean not on [our] own understanding'. My three-year-old granddaughter reminded me of this spiritual lesson. Sometimes I need to change the way I'm looking at a situation. I need to ask for his perspective. He is the only one who sees and knows how all the pieces fit together.

Prayer: *Dear Lord, thank you for your wisdom. Help us to see as you see and to trust your vision. Amen.*

Thought for the day: How might I change my perspective to see as God sees?

Lynne Mirabella (Georgia, USA)

Uniquely created

Read Genesis 1:20–31
God created humans in his image, in the image of God he created them; male and female he created them.
Genesis 1:27 (NRSV)

On a recent walk, I spotted an oak leaf lying among maple leaves. The fallen beige leaf stood out on the golden carpet of maple leaves. Its rounded lobes contrasted with the sharp points of the other leaves surrounding it. Still, together, the leaves were beautiful.

How often do we notice someone who is different? Skin colour, style of clothing, hairstyle, age and other features may set them apart from the crowd. Maybe *we* are the unique people where we work, live or go to school. Sometimes people stand out, and that's just fine.

God creates each person with unique gifts and abilities. Even though we are different from one another, we all bear the image of God. Together with one another and the Divine, we collaborate to establish justice, make peace and promote love.

Some people may desire that everyone conform to the same appearance, style or belief, but God creates variety. The diversity of the natural world and humanity bring wonder and joy in their myriad expressions of God's creativity. Let us embrace God's work of love and our calling to celebrate that labour.

Prayer: *God who delights in diversity, thank you for creating each of us. Help us to appreciate the variety you have made and to treat every person with kindness. In Christ's name. Amen.*

Thought for the day: I will give thanks for how God has made me unique.

Marty Toepke-Floyd (North Dakota, USA)

A prayer for help

Read Psalm 20

May the Lord answer you when you are in distress; may the name of the God of Jacob protect you. May he send you help from the sanctuary and grant you support from Zion.
Psalm 20:1–2 (NIV)

It is a quiet, peaceful winter morning. The sky is still dark, and my children are asleep. Before the day dawns, I take a moment to thank God for a new day and ask God to help me through it.

My prayer for help reminds me of the prayers in Psalm 20. When King David was about to head to battle with his troops, the people of Israel prayed for his protection. David's victory meant life and freedom for his people, so they sang: 'May we shout for joy over your victory and lift up our banners in the name of our God' (v. 5).

David experienced God's protection as he fought and defeated Goliath. So David responded by saying, 'Now this I know: the Lord gives victory to his anointed. He answers him from his heavenly sanctuary with the victorious power of his right hand' (v. 6).

As the day dawns and the cares of the day await us, we can trust in the name of the Lord. The Lord will answer us when we are in distress – protecting us, sending help and granting support.

Prayer: *Dear Lord, help us to rely on you and trust you even when we have lost hope. Help us to see that you are our ever-present help in trouble. Amen.*

Thought for the day: I can trust God today and every day.

Yana Ibragimova (North Gyeongsang, South Korea)

A season of change

Read Ecclesiastes 3:1–8

For everything there is a season and a time for every matter under heaven.

Ecclesiastes 3:1 (NRSV)

When I began my teaching career many years ago, I was responsible for decorating the bulletin board in the front entrance of the school. The board needed to be appealing, inspiring and creative. It would also require a lot of time and preparation. Many times, I was unable to complete the board in one day, so I put up a sign that said, 'Pardon me! I'm changing; I'm a work in progress!'

Since my retirement, I have experienced many challenges and changes in my life. I can't do the things I used to do; at times I feel inadequate. I wonder whether I am still able to do God's work. Can God still use me? In this season of my life, despite my fears, I know I still need God's pardon and grace. Yes, I am still a work in progress.

Then I think about the scripture that reads, 'The one who began a good work in you will continue to complete it until the day of Jesus Christ' (Philippians 1:6). I thank God that although I may be changing, God never changes. What a comfort it is to know that God still heals, still restores, still gives us whatever we need to change from our way to God's way!

Prayer: *O Lord, help us understand that change is a necessary part of life. Help us to use change in a positive way for our good and the good of others. Amen.*

Thought for the day: Changes can bring unexpected blessings.

Tryphena Rhue Taylor (South Carolina, USA)

God will provide

Read Philippians 4:10–13

Surely I know the plans I have for you, says the Lord, plans for your welfare and not for harm, to give you a future with hope.
Jeremiah 29:11 (NRSV)

I knew I would soon experience financial hardship. The second year of graduate school was approaching, and payment on a large loan was awaiting me. Interest rates and fees for tuition loans were high, and I could not find a stable job for the summer.

Growing up, I always heard 'God will provide' but never thought much of it because I had been blessed not to have to face financial difficulty. But now that this dark cloud loomed over me, I felt vulnerable, helpless and desperate. I found myself reaching out to God for help but realised God was not going to provide me with an instant, miraculous solution to my problem.

Soon enough, I was offered an opportunity as a paid musician for weekly church services. Then I found a scholarship to apply for. I also held a large garage sale. I discovered that God was providing me with small, open doors and nourishing my creativity to find new ways of earning what I needed.

Despite lingering worries, I found myself happier than ever after deciding to turn to God. I began trusting God to provide. I know that God will continue to provide in unexpected ways and will always be my source of strength.

Prayer: *Dear God, may we ask for help when we need it and open our eyes to what you have already given us. Amen.*

Thought for the day: God will provide, but not always how or when I expect.

June Chung (New Jersey, USA)

An unbroken chain

Read Psalm 22:3–5
*Remember the days of old; consider the generations long past.
Ask your father and he will tell you, your elders, and they will
explain to you.*
Deuteronomy 32:7 (NIV)

One summer my friend and I stayed a week in Kirkwall, a port in the Ork-
ney Islands, northeast of Scotland. What is remarkable about this small
town is the magnificent St Magnus Cathedral from the twelfth century.
It was founded by the Norwegian Earl Rognvald.

On Sunday, we went to the worship service. The large church was
almost completely full. While waiting for the service to start, I looked up at
the medieval arches above us and thought of all the generations that had
worshipped our Lord in this church – from the days of the Vikings to today.

There is an unbroken chain of people seeking the Lord for guidance,
support and comfort. I was reminded of this at St Magnus Cathedral, but
it is the same at my small local church. God is the same everywhere. And
together we seek the Lord.

Prayer: *Dear Lord, thank you for your grace and love and for the
generations of believers who have shared the gospel with their
neighbours. In the name of Jesus we pray. Amen.*

Thought for the day: I am part of an unbroken chain of witnesses
seeking God and sharing the good news.

Øystein Brinch (Oslo, Norway)

A living faith

Read Deuteronomy 15:7–11
*As the body without the spirit is dead, so faith without works
is dead also.*
James 2:26 (KJV)

I knew my friend was going through a hard time. She was out of work
and had three children to feed. I imagined a gift of a few groceries might
help to ease her burden. So I headed to the supermarket and picked up
a few essentials for her and her family. When I delivered the groceries,
her look of surprise was quickly replaced by one of sheer gratitude. As
she placed the items in her near-empty cabinets, she said, 'You know,
I'll take these over "thoughts and prayers" any day.' That moment was
a wonderful lesson for me.

How many times, after learning of someone's hardship, do I promise
to keep them in my thoughts or include them in my prayers? I know the
right things to say, but do I act on them? We must pray for those in need,
of course, but people also need tangible help. A bag of groceries, a ride
to a doctor's appointment, an afternoon of babysitting so that a weary
parent can rest – these are simple ways we can meet an immediate need.

Today's quoted scripture reminds us that 'faith without works is dead'.
When we put our faith into action, our faith is alive. In what ways can we
show our living faith to those in need? Even a small act of kindness can
make a big difference.

Prayer: *Generous God, show us how to put our faith into action, and
give us the strength and courage to follow through. Amen.*

Thought for the day: God encourages me to help others through
prayer *and* action.

Monica A. Andermann (New York, USA)

A grateful heart

Read Ephesians 5:15–20

Always give thanks to God the Father for everything in the name of our Lord Jesus Christ.
Ephesians 5:20 (CEB)

For weeks I had been battling feelings of stress, irritation and anger. I felt frustrated with everyone and everything. While getting ready for work one day, I told God I didn't know why my attitude was so bad, but I wanted to change it. I asked for God's help to reveal what I needed to do to reverse course. One word immediately settled into my heart: gratitude.

I spent the remainder of the morning and my commute to work expressing gratitude to God for big and small things. I thanked God for clean water to bathe in; for the scrambled eggs I enjoyed for breakfast; for a car that works; for my sweet dogs who make me laugh; for God's mercies that are new every day; and for so much more. As I continued to express thankfulness, my sour attitude became sweeter and sweeter.

Today's scripture reading reminds us to make music to the Lord in our hearts and to give thanks to God for everything. When we practise gratitude and centre our hearts on thankfulness, we not only honour God, but we are more joyful, peaceful and loving.

Prayer: *Dear God, help us to nurture within ourselves a heart of gratitude and thanksgiving towards you. Amen.*

Thought for the day: A grateful heart honours God and gives me joy and peace.

Emily Marszalek (Idaho, USA)

Eager to learn

Read Acts 8:26–40

Every scripture is inspired by God and is useful for teaching,
for showing mistakes, for correcting, and for training character,
so that the person who belongs to God can be equipped to do
everything that is good.
2 Timothy 3:16–17 (CEB)

I enjoy teaching mathematics – a subject that some of my students don't like. I try to teach them using methods that are interesting and fun.

When Philip saw that the eunuch from Ethiopia was reading scripture, Philip enthusiastically greeted him and asked if he understood what he was reading. Philip responded to the eunuch's interest in scripture and used that precious time to preach the gospel of Jesus Christ to him. The eunuch eagerly wanted to learn and listened to Philip's teachings and explanations. Philip taught with enthusiasm so that the eunuch wanted to be baptised immediately and become a follower of Jesus.

When others express interest, it is a good opportunity to introduce them to Jesus. We can emulate Philip's attitude and eagerly share the good news of Christ.

Prayer: *Holy Teacher, thank you for teachers who inspire us with their enthusiasm and passion. Help us to share your good news with those we meet today. Amen.*

Thought for the day: My joy in God's good news has the power to inspire others.

Rosta Merry Gultom (West Java, Indonesia)

Sparrow's nest

Read Matthew 10:26–31
'Don't be afraid; you are worth more than many sparrows.'
Matthew 10:31 (NIV)

In 2016, my wife of 53 years suffered a stroke. Memory loss and balance problems reduced a once vibrant, active, social, travel-loving woman to someone who needed help with even the most basic daily tasks. Fortunately, I was still healthy and strong and could care for her. We moved into a senior-housing facility. What we once thought was a bright future suddenly darkened, but we put our trust in the Lord as we faced the uncertainties and challenges of a new way of living.

When we got settled in our unit, we noted that all the rooms in the facility had names. Ours was named 'Sparrow's Nest', and we were reassured of the Lord's care by recalling Matthew 10:31 – 'Don't be afraid; you are worth more than many sparrows.'

Daily we are aware of God's blessing that in our senior years my wife and I are together – and that each new day God's caring eye is on us.

Prayer: *Heavenly Father, thank you for the blessings of our younger years and for your continuing love and care as we face the future in our older years. Amen.*

Thought for the day: Even in uncertain times, I know Jesus watches over me.

Narciso S. Albarracin Jr. (Ohio, USA)

A straight line

Read Proverbs 4:20–27

I press on towards the goal, towards the prize of the heavenly call of God in Christ Jesus.
Philippians 3:14 (NRSV)

In college, I had a job working in a forest, setting up boundaries for large entomology study plots that needed to be measured and oriented precisely so that all the plots would be the same. However, you cannot walk very far in a straight line through a forest – a tree, bush, rock or other obstacle will always be in your way.

The best technique is to aim a compass in the direction you want to go. Then identify a distinctive tree straight ahead in the distance that is visible above the surrounding vegetation. Moving forward involves alternately watching where you put your feet and checking that your goal tree is still straight ahead. When you must go around an obstacle, you reorient yourself by locating and heading towards your goal tree.

My Christian journey reminds me of walking a straight line in the forest. There are many things to enjoy and interesting sights and sounds to distract me. There are obstacles to work around. I can trip if I am not careful. And at times, the view of my goal may be temporarily blocked. However, I walk without fear of getting lost because God is with me. I have turned my back on my past life. The Bible is my compass, pointing the way. And prayer keeps my eyes on Jesus and me heading towards him.

Prayer: *Creator God, thank you for the beauty of your world. May we always hear your call and follow you. Amen.*

Thought for the day: I will keep my eyes on Jesus by praying and studying the Bible.

Mary Neumann (Georgia, USA)

In the Lord's footsteps

Read 2 Timothy 1:1–14

It is the Lord who goes before you. He will be with you; he will not fail you or forsake you. Do not fear or be dismayed.
Deuteronomy 31:8 (NRSV)

In India we rarely see snow. So when I visited Dallas, Texas, in the United States, I was excited to see a snowfall. I wanted to walk on the snow, but I kept slipping and falling. It appeared soft on top but was slippery beneath. I was determined and walked very slowly. The streets were empty, but I spotted the footprints of someone who had gone ahead. Walking in their footprints was much easier. I thanked God for the person who had left them.

I realised that Jesus also has done the difficult job of making the first footprints for others to follow. So did Timothy and those who followed Christ. In one of Paul's letters to Timothy, he shares his knowledge and experiences. Paul leads by both example and teaching and encourages Timothy to do the same. He says in 2 Timothy 2:2, 'What you have heard from me through many witnesses entrust to faithful people who will be able to teach others as well.'

The beautiful part is that, centuries later, Christ is here to lead and direct our footsteps. As I follow Christ's footsteps, I pray that I, too, will leave footsteps that make it easier for others to follow.

Prayer: *Dear Lord Jesus, thank you for making paths for us to follow. Guide our steps as we move forward in faith each day. Amen.*

Thought for the day: The paths I make help others follow Christ.

Bella Pillai (Uttar Pradesh, India)

Four anchors

Read Psalm 107:23–32

Fearing that we would be dashed against the rocks, they dropped four anchors from the stern.
Acts 27:29 (NIV)

Many years ago, I was caught in a force 9 gale at sea. The waves were enormous, with strong and gusting winds that made the ferry pitch from side to side. All I could do was sit tight, literally.

Sometimes in life, we have metaphorical gales that hit us – circumstances or events that knock us off our feet. I experienced one such time when I was diagnosed with cancer. The diagnosis took my breath away, and over the next few months, through surgery and treatment, the storm was relentless.

During that time, Acts 27:29 became very meaningful to me. It is one of several Bible passages describing a storm at sea. In this one, the storm is so bad that the sailors drop four anchors to prevent the ship crashing against rocks. I too learnt to drop four 'anchors'. The first was to keep recalling all the times God had provided for me in the past. The second was to remind myself of God's character and goodness. The third was to meditate on verses of scripture, saying them aloud and savouring them. Finally, the fourth 'anchor' was to keep praising and thanking God for being faithful, both in times gone by and in what I was currently facing.

These four simple things kept me anchored in God, and like literal storms, my personal storm eventually passed. I have continued to hold on to those four anchors many times since.

Prayer: *Thank you, Father, that we can anchor ourselves in you, firm and secure in whatever storms we are facing today. Amen.*

Thought for the day: God remains faithful in every season.

Caroline Mansell (England, United Kingdom)

Serving where you are

Read Jeremiah 29:4–7

'Build houses and settle down; plant gardens and eat what they produce… Seek the peace and prosperity of the city to which I have carried you into exile. Pray to the Lord for it, because if it prospers, you too will prosper.'
Jeremiah 29:5, 7 (NIV)

A year ago, my husband and I moved to be closer to our two daughters. In making this move, I retired from my job as a professor. I had loved the interaction with colleagues and students, the research, and the challenge of teaching. So I planned to find volunteer work that felt challenging to fill my days.

Our parents, then in their mid-90s, chose to move with us and moved into a nearby senior-living facility. My husband and I spent much time at the facility, so I got to know the other residents. I began listening to their stories, remembering their birthdays and teaching a weekly Bible study. After a while, I realised that I was again joyfully interacting with people, researching and teaching right where God had put me.

In Jeremiah 29, the prophet relayed God's word to the exiles in Babylon, telling them to assimilate into their new home. They were called to help the city prosper by using their skills to plant gardens and build houses. Jeremiah urged them to find meaning and good work right where God put them.

Prayer: *Heavenly Father, change is hard. Help us to trust that you have good work for us to do wherever you put us. Amen.*

Thought for the day: God can use me right where I am.

Lori Carter (Washington, USA)

Forgiveness and freedom

Read Genesis 50:15–21

'Is not this the kind of fasting I have chosen: to loose the chains of injustice and untie the cords of the yoke, to set the oppressed free?'
Isaiah 58:6 (NIV)

I have fond memories from my childhood. It was great, but it also had challenges. I have five siblings, and I am the oldest. Conflict was ever-present between us. But we were young and forgiveness came quickly – usually in a matter of minutes.

Children have a lot to teach us in this regard. It is easy for them to forgive and forget. It is no wonder that Christ told his disciples that they must become like children to inherit the kingdom of God (see Matthew 18:3). To be free is to have the innocence of a child – to find the willingness to forgive and forget like a child.

The Bible offers many examples of how we can let go of malice and choose to forgive. Choosing forgiveness releases us from the bondage of sin and allows us to embrace the innocence of a child.

Prayer: *Dear Father God, help us to forgive others just as you forgive us. In Jesus' name. Amen.*

Thought for the day: When I am quick to forgive, I am living out Jesus' instruction to become like a child.

Marius Bâgu (Vaslui, Romania)

Comfort and help

Read 2 Corinthians 1:3–7

Praise be to the God and Father of our Lord Jesus Christ… who comforts us in all our troubles, so that we can comfort those in any trouble with the comfort we ourselves receive from God.
2 Corinthians 1:3–4 (NIV)

I stood outside the hospital room where my father lay dying. As tears ran down my cheeks, relentless, crashing waves of grief threatened to crush me in a flood of emotions. My heart cried out to God in that brutal moment: 'Please, God, please! Please, help my dad. Please, help me.'

As my tears continued to flow, I felt the warmth of God's presence around me. God answered my desperate prayer and gave me the peace I needed to return to my father's bedside. A few days later my dad passed away, but God continued to comfort me with the knowledge that my father was with Jesus and that Dad's pain was gone.

God now helps me to reach out with compassion as I speak to friends who are experiencing their own losses. I pray for them, asking God to provide them with the comfort God gave to me. I speak with empathy from having walked through painful loss. I talk about the kindness of God, who is tender to the broken-hearted, and I share scripture that speaks of God's care, comfort and presence. When there are no words to say, I simply offer a peaceful presence for those who are hurting. God can bring good out of painful seasons by teaching us to comfort others.

Prayer: *Heavenly Father, thank you for comforting us in life's storms. Help us share the comfort we have received with others who are suffering. In the name of Jesus. Amen.*

Thought for the day: God comforts me in painful seasons so that I can comfort others.

Barbara Culley (Washington, USA)

Paying attention

Read Isaiah 58:5–11

Those who give to the poor will lack nothing, but those who close their eyes to them receive many curses.
Proverbs 28:27 (NIV)

My husband and I pulled into a rest area to eat lunch on our way home from a trip. An older woman sat near the restrooms, holding a cardboard sign saying, 'Please help. Need gas money.' She stared at the ground, shoulders slumped forward. People passed her on their way to the restrooms, but nobody even glanced at her. It was like she was invisible.

She was limping towards her car when I handed her some cash with a quick, 'God bless you.' I started to turn away when she said, 'Would you pray for me?' I stopped and looked into her eyes. 'Please pray that I can find a job,' she said. I promised that I would and then impulsively added, 'Would you like me to pray right now?' I had never done anything like that before, and I'm not sure what made me say it, but the woman nodded.

I asked God to help her to find a job and the assistance she needed. It felt awkward, but afterward the woman smiled and thanked me. 'I know God will take care of me,' she said. As I walked away, I marvelled at her faith. Would I still trust God if I had to beg for money? I vowed to remember this encounter and pay attention to each person I meet.

Prayer: *Dear God, open our eyes to see those around us and offer help as you lead us. Amen.*

Thought for the day: What immediate need can I meet for someone today?

Susan Thogerson Maas (Oregon, USA)

The power of forgiveness

Read Luke 15:11–24

The son said to him, 'Father, I have sinned against heaven and against you. I am no longer worthy to be called your son.' But the father said to his servants, 'Quick! Bring the best robe and put it on him. Put a ring on his finger and sandals on his feet.'
Luke 15:21–22 (NIV)

I struggled growing up in poverty and without my father in my life, even though I knew he was alive. My life took a turn for the worse, and I didn't believe in anything. At school I started to isolate myself; I didn't want any friends because of the pain I was feeling from my father's rejection. I started to do bad things to numb the pain, but the hole grew deeper. I wanted my father to feel the hurt I was going through, and I wished a lot of bad things on him so I could feel better about myself. But the pain started to affect everyone around me, including those I love dearly.

One day I noticed how toxic I was being. I realised that I wasn't the victim that I thought I was; I was also now a perpetrator of hate. My journey took another turn. I started to pray. I have learned not to dwell on the pain other people cause me. By learning to forgive and forget, I have found healing and a joyous life.

Prayer: *Father God, may we focus on you and know you deeply so that we may act like Jesus, forgiving others as you forgive us. Amen.*

Thought for the day: Forgiveness is the key to contentment.

Percy Mangwedi (Gauteng, South Africa)

God at work

Read Philippians 2:12–18

It is God who is at work in you, enabling you both to will and to work for his good pleasure.
Philippians 2:13 (NRSV)

I found myself in a hospital bed, recovering from a stroke and thinking, *If I can just get through this.* Thankfully, I had no paralysis or changes in my speech, but I did lose some peripheral vision. After eight days, I was able to go home. But there were many changes. I was bumping into things and had to teach myself how to manoeuvre all over again. But I got through it.

When we experience challenges, often we immediately think, *I just have to get through this.* We always want the trial to end and a good, carefree life to resume. But as I reflect on the trials of my life, I notice that the toughest times are typically when I can focus on God the best. I think of life's hardships as construction zones in which we can rely on God in greater ways than we ever have before. My stroke affected me physically, but it also helped me spiritually. I have learned to thank God in all circumstances.

God is always with us, and what a joy it is to experience God's peace in the trials we face! We need not fear the construction zones of life because they are opportunities for our faith to grow firm in the one who created us.

Prayer: *Dear God, thank you for being at work in our lives. Help us to trust that it is for our good and your glory. Amen.*

Thought for the day: I can trust that God is at work in the construction zones of my life.

Susan K. Shumway (Ohio, USA)

Finish today

Read Psalm 118:19–24

I trusted in thee, O Lord: I said, Thou art my God. My times are in thy hand.
Psalm 31:14–15 (KJV)

Recently I was reading through journals I kept when our grandsons were young. I wrote down something my grandson Seth said when he was six years old. I had asked him what he would be doing in the next few days, and he replied, 'Actually, Grammie, I'm just going to finish today, and then I'll do tomorrow.' I smiled as I recalled this conversation, and I was struck by the wisdom in this young boy's words. He wasn't looking back at yesterday or making a definite plan for tomorrow. He was simply finishing today.

As an adult it is necessary to schedule my time, and I strive to make wise plans for the future. And yet, Seth's words reminded me of the importance of appreciating the present moment. The present is 'the day which the Lord hath made', and each day is an opportunity to rejoice and be glad in God's provision (see Psalm 118:24).

Sometimes I can run too far ahead in my planning. In doing so, I run the risk of missing today's blessings and experiencing unnecessary anxiety. Instead, I want to balance wise planning with a focus on finishing each day in a way that will please God. How comforting it is to trust in the One who provides my daily bread and to know that my time is in God's hands!

Prayer: *Dear Father, help us to have childlike faith, entrusting our days to you. Amen.*

Thought for the day: Today I will focus on the present and look to Jesus, the author and finisher of my faith (see Hebrews 12:2).

Sandra Sullivan (West Virginia, USA)

Highest calling

Read Matthew 25:31–46

*'The King will reply, "Truly I tell you, whatever you did for one of
the least of these brothers and sisters of mine, you did for me."'*
Matthew 25:40 (NIV)

Tucked away on a peaceful street, our church stands far from the places
where the rich and powerful dwell. But we have a wonderful opportunity
being close to those who suffer most – people without houses, with addictions, in prison, grieving. Every day, we encounter these children of God
who are often overlooked. When we serve them, we serve Christ himself.

The noise of daily life can lead us to focus only on our own needs and
comfort. But Jesus urges us to look beyond ourselves and our worries. He
invites us to see where people most need hope and healing. He is waiting
for us there – in the widow's tears, in the father's trembling hands, in the
child's hungry cry. Serving the poor and wounded is our highest calling
as Christians; it is how we express Christ's love.

Our church may not impress the world with our money or status. But
we can offer something priceless: God's presence through our simple acts
of service. As we feed the hungry and visit the lonely, we shine Christ's
light. The world may not see it, but that doesn't matter. Loving those
whom Jesus named 'the least of these' is the core of our calling.

Prayer: *Loving God, open our eyes to see you in the faces of those who
are forgotten and hurting. Lead us each day to live out Christ's love
through simple acts of compassion. Amen.*

Thought for the day: To find God, I will look for those in need.

Duy Khang Nguyen (Ho Chi Minh City, Vietnam)

Unprepared

Read Psalm 19:7–14

*Some trust in chariots, and some in horses: but we will remember
the name of the Lord our God.*

Psalm 20:7 (KJV)

I recently applied for a job that required a written examination. I would
have one hour to answer 60 questions. However, no information was
given as to the kind of questions that would be on the exam. So I did
some online research, and I borrowed a book from the library. When
I started the exam, though, neither the online research nor the library
book had given me the information I needed. I simply had to do the best
I could in the time allotted.

Life is like that, isn't it? We wish we could study for future tests and
trials; but when we are plunged into some unexpected circumstance,
we find there is little we could have done to prepare. No comprehensive
guide exists on how to survive after a spouse's infidelity or how to live
joyfully when suffering from depression. There are few stages of life we
will go into feeling completely prepared.

So what do we do? We trust God's love and guidance. We can strengthen
ourselves by reading and following God's word, by spending time in worship and prayer. And when unexpected exams of life come, we simply do
the best we can. Above all, we can trust that the one who has our best
interests at heart will help us navigate every test that comes our way.

Prayer: *Dear God, help us to know without doubt that all things are
in your hands, even in times of severe testing. Amen.*

Thought for the day: Instead of trusting only in my own efforts,
I can trust in God's wisdom and direction.

Bonita Jewel (California, USA)

I won't let you go

Read Psalm 73:23–26
I cling to you; your right hand upholds me.
Psalm 63:8 (NIV)

I volunteer as an usher at our local theatre, showing people to their seats and clearing up after the performance. Recently an elderly lady, on coming down the steps after the performance, misplaced her footing and toppled backwards and fell to the ground. Helping her to her feet, I realised she was still very unsteady. As I kept hold of her, I found myself reassuring her by saying, 'It's okay. I'll not let you go.' I ensured she was able to negotiate the one further step and go safely on her way. She had to trust that I would do what I said and that I would take care of her.

There is much in the Bible about God's hands and arms – his holding of us, his keeping of us, his taking of our hand and his guiding of us. God is unfailingly faithful in watching over us and in leading us on the right path. He won't let us go. Our response is to put our trust in him.

Prayer: *Dear Lord, in you we put our trust this day. Thank you that in your tender care, you will not let us go. We pray as Jesus taught us, 'Our Father in heaven, may your name be revered as holy. May your kingdom come. May your will be done on earth as it is in heaven. Give us today our daily bread. And forgive us our debts, as we also have forgiven our debtors. And do not bring us to the time of trial, but rescue us from the evil one' (Matthew 6:9–13, NRSV). Amen.*

Thought for the day: 'Immediately Jesus reached out his hand and caught him' (Matthew 14:31).

Hilary Allen (England, United Kingdom)

Growing to maturity

Read Luke 13:6–9

Let this endurance complete its work so that you may be fully mature, complete, and lacking in nothing.
James 1:4 (CEB)

My orange lilies failed to bloom for almost five years. Initially, I had planted the bulbs in a flowerpot. Then I transplanted them into the ground. Two or three years passed and, disappointingly, there were no lilies. I repotted them and waited and watched for another year or two, but still no blooms appeared.

Then early one May I noticed a stalk protruding from the pot – the beginnings of a bud at its tip. A week or so later, the first flower appeared in its full, fiery splendour. Finally! I consulted the internet to find out why it had taken my lilies so long to bloom, and I was surprised to learn that the problem could be either that the soil they were in was too shallow or that the bulbs were not mature enough.

Often we can feel like my lilies or the fruitless fig tree in today's scripture reading. Even if we have been Christians for many years, at times our lives may fail to produce the fruit of the Spirit (see Galatians 5:22–23). It can seem as if we are wasting the soil of our salvation. But when we take time to nurture faith through studying and applying God's word, praying continuously and spending time with other believers, our walk with Christ will deepen and develop and yield a harvest that brings glory to God.

Prayer: *Dear God, transform our hearts by the power of your Holy Spirit so that we may be fruitful witnesses of your goodness and grace. Amen.*

Thought for the day: What actions am I taking to nurture my spiritual growth?

Arlene Timber-Henry (St. Maarten)

Bread of life

Read Micah 6:6–8

He has told you, O mortal, what is good, and what does the Lord require of you but to do justice and to love kindness and to walk humbly with your God?

Micah 6:8 (NRSV)

I was sorting through papers and noticed a simple and delicious recipe for Irish soda bread that had been given to me by a friend. I decided to bake it for dinner: 'Mix four cups of flour, one teaspoon of baking soda, a heaping teaspoon of salt, and two cups of buttermilk. Roll into a ball, place on a greased pie tin, and bake at 375 degrees for 50 minutes.' I inhaled the heady aroma as the bread baked. A thick slice of warm, buttered bread was my reward for following the recipe.

If only life were as simple as following a recipe, I mused. Then I recalled today's scripture verse that instructs us to do justice, love kindness and walk humbly with God. This basic recipe from God's word says to fill the mixing bowl of our lives with honesty and integrity, spoon in a mixture of grace and mercy, and complete the process with an intimate but humble relationship with God. Bake the ingredients with love, and the result will be a life that is pleasing to God.

Prayer: *Dear Father, teach us to study your simple truths, to stir them into our hearts and to share them with others. Amen.*

Thought for the day: I will strive to do justice, love kindness, and walk humbly with God.

Mary Korf (Oklahoma, USA)

Small group questions

Wednesday 7 May

1 When have you experienced an illness or injury that hindered your ability to serve or work in the way you had in the past? What did you do? In what new ways did you serve or work?

2 When have you witnessed someone's ministry being strengthened after a setback? What happened? Why do you think the setback ultimately empowered their efforts?

3 Do you ever feel that your best days are behind you? Why or why not? What helps you remain encouraged that your contributions to the world are valuable?

4 Do you have a fresh, forward-focused vision? If so, what is it? If not, how will you ask God for guidance? What will keep you motivated to pursue that vision?

5 How does it encourage you to know that God is never done with us? How does this knowledge help you look forward to what is ahead?

Wednesday 14 May

1 Recall a time when you found it difficult to appreciate someone's good qualities. Why was it difficult for you? What helped you to see the good in them?

2 How does prayer help you to view others with compassion rather than judgement? Why do you think praying helps us to release bitterness and negativity?

3 When have you found it challenging to meet a haughty spirit with humility and gentleness? What spiritual practices help you remain grace-filled and loving even when dealing with people who challenge you?

4 What scripture passages most encourage you to love others and continue doing good work? Why do they encourage you? How do you keep these verses at the forefront of your mind each day?

5 Who has extended grace to you recently? What did they do? What did their actions teach you about extending grace to others?

Wednesday 21 May

1 Have you ever met someone who has made it their life's mission to share the gospel? What is their story? How does their example inspire you?

2 How does the story of the Samaritan woman encourage you to tell others about Christ? Who else in scripture encourages you to share the message of Christ with those around you?

3 When have you shied away from sharing your faith with someone? Why? What prayers and spiritual practices help you boldly share the good news of Christ?

4 Who has shared their faith with you in a meaningful way? How did they share it? How do you strive to do the same?

5 In what ways can you share the gospel with your community today? How can you share the gospel more broadly? Name three ways in which you can share God's love with others this week.

Wednesday 28 May

1 Do you make New Year's resolutions? Why or why not? If so, do you find them helpful? Do you engage in any other practices around the new year?

2 Would you ever consider starting a gratitude list like today's writer did? How do you think making such a list can impact your faith?

3 How does focusing on your blessings shift your mindset and change the way you treat others? Why do you think gratitude causes these shifts?

4   Do you find it easy or challenging to entrust your concerns to God? Why? How does trusting God with your concerns enable your heart to grow?

5   Do you view every moment as a blessing? Why or why not? How might your attitude and your actions change if you chose to celebrate every moment you are granted?

Wednesday 4 June

1   What do you do when you struggle to sleep? Where do you find peace on sleepless nights?

2   What sounds of nature do you find most peaceful and comforting? How do these sounds remind you that God is speaking to you?

3   When have you received a message from God that helped you get through your day? What was the message? How did it help you? How are you encouraged to know you don't have to face life alone?

4   Do you ever get too busy to listen to what God is telling you? What do you miss out on when you stop listening to God? How can you become better at making time to listen to God?

5   In what ways do you strive to be ready to respond whenever and wherever God calls? What does it look like to be ready? How do you respond when God speaks to you?

Wednesday 11 June

1   Have you ever used something as a guide, only to find that it was not accurate or helpful? What did you learn from this experience?

2   Who has been a role model for you? How did their example influence your life?

3   Do you think that it is good to have role models? Why or why not?

4   Why do you think aligning with other people can make it easy to go in a direction we don't intend? What helps you to stay on the path you desire?

5   What does it look like to follow Jesus' example and to align our lives with him? What can we do to be better followers of Christ?

Wednesday 18 June

1   When you experience betrayal and pain, do you turn to scripture for guidance? Why or why not? What verses have been the most influential for you in such situations?

2   Do you find it easy to forgive when you have been hurt? How does God's forgiveness of us change the way you forgive others?

3   What scripture verses most remind you of the importance of forgiveness? How do these verses help you when you are tempted to hold onto resentment?

4   When has prayer healed your heart? What was the process like? What else has helped you heal?

5   Call to mind a relationship that needs healing. What prayers, scripture verses, spiritual practices and actions can you take to move towards healing?

Wednesday 25 June

1   Do you practise an exercise regimen? If so, how does that regimen enrich your life? If not, what other daily regimens do you practise?

2   Where do you find time in the busyness of your day to reflect on and talk to God? How does this time strengthen your connection with God?

3   What aspects of creation most remind you of God's presence and care? How do you take time to notice and appreciate these parts of creation?

4   When has God given you a message through creation? How did you receive this message? What did you do after receiving it?

5 How do you remain connected to God no matter your circumstances? What spiritual practices help you remain close to God?

Wednesday 2 July

1 When have you found that observing nature was not as peaceful as you expected? Why? What did you learn from your observations?

2 Recall a time when you knew there was enough for all, yet you still witnessed fighting and discontent. Why do you think this happened? What was the outcome?

3 Do you find yourself growing weary from the conflict and disunion in the world? Why or why not? What helps you find peace in times of conflict?

4 What scripture verses help you remember that Christ will return and bring healing, justice and peace? Why are these verses helpful for you? How do you cling to them when you feel disheartened?

5 How do you think it will feel in Christ's new creation? What do you think will be different from our current world? What do you think will remain?

Wednesday 9 July

1 When have you been cared for by or provided care for a loved one? What was the experience like? How did that caregiving impact your relationship?

2 When has a mutual love for Christ strengthened a relationship of yours? Why did it do so? How does your love for Christ impact all your relationships?

3 How does your love for God and for others help you overcome challenges? How does your faith help you to cherish moments of joy with those you love?

4　Think of an important relationship in your life. What relationship in scripture most resembles your experience? What can you learn from the relationship in the Bible?

5　What relationships have been the greatest challenge for you? Why? What relationships have been the greatest gifts to you? How do they draw you closer to God?

Wednesday 16 July

1　When have you arrived somewhere only to find a place completely different from what you were expecting? What happened? How did you respond?

2　Recall a time when a location or situation seemed dry and lifeless but was actually teeming with life. How did you realise it was not as barren as it seemed?

3　When have you been unaware of God's creative power at work in a situation, only to notice it after pausing to look around? What brought it to your awareness? How did noticing God's creativity change your view of the situation?

4　What scripture passages most remind you of God's ability to bring beauty and life into anything? How do these passages encourage you?

5　What areas of your life feel barren and dry? Why? What prayers and spiritual practices help you to welcome God's creative and rejuvenating power in this part of your life?

Wednesday 23 July

1　Do you struggle to know what to pray? Why or why not? What do you do when you don't know what to pray?

2　Does scripture help you when you don't have the words to pray? In what ways? Do you ever pray using words from scripture?

3 What is your favourite scripture verse? Why is it your favourite? How do you use this verse in your daily spiritual practice?

4 Have you ever simply prayed Jesus' name? If so, how did the prayer impact you? If not, have you ever considered praying his name? Why or why not?

5 Who has taught you how to pray? Whom have you taught how to pray? What are the most meaningful prayer practices you have learned from other believers?

Wednesday 30 July

1 When have you had more than you needed? What did you do with the extra? Describe what happened.

2 Recall a time when you witnessed a diverse group coming together for a cause. What was the outcome? What did you learn from that experience?

3 What is the significance for you of everyone's being welcome at God's table? How are you encouraged by that fact? How do you make sure others know they are welcome there too?

4 When have you received a seemingly simple gift that made a significant difference for you? When have you been transformed by giving a simple gift?

5 Who in your community needs your help today? How can you help them? How will you remain open to the needs of those around you moving forward?

Wednesday 6 August

1 When have you felt alone? Why did you feel that way? How did feeling alone impact your actions?

2 Do the laughter and opinions of others change the way you feel about your choices? Why or why not? What do you do when people laugh at or criticise you?

3 Recall a time when you prayed for strength before doing something. Did God provide the strength you needed? What happened?

4 Why is it so easy to end up doing things that make us unhappy just to please other people? How does it feel when you do this? What would happen if you stopped doing it?

5 In what ways does God's love and presence give you confidence? How does leaning on God help you make choices that make you happy, even if others mock you?

Wednesday 13 August

1 Who in your life is in need of help? What are some tangible ways you can assist them this week?

2 Do you ever feel like you need more than just thoughts and prayers? Why or why not? How does physical support feel different from thoughts and prayers in times of need?

3 When you know someone needs help, what prayer practices help you pray for them? How do you then follow that prayer with action?

4 Describe a time when you witnessed a small act of kindness that made a big difference. Why do you think that act was so meaningful? What did you learn from it?

5 What scripture verses most encourage you to pray and offer physical help? How can you keep these verses at the forefront of your mind as you look for ways to help others?

Wednesday 20 August

1 Recall a time when you made a big life change. What was it like? How did you adjust to the change?

2 When have you found unexpected ways to serve others and do what makes you happy? What did you do? How did this change your outlook?

3 How are you encouraged by the story in Jeremiah 29? In what ways does it inspire you to find meaning and good work wherever you are?

4 When have you experienced God guiding you to good work? Had you anticipated working in that way? How did God guide you?

5 Who in your life best exemplifies serving where God has put them? How do they do so? What can you learn from their example?

Wednesday 27 August

1 Have you ever had the opportunity to be close to those who suffer the most? If so, where? How did you show them God's love? If not, what are some ways you can draw closer to those suffering and care for them?

2 Why do you think it's so easy to focus only on our own needs and comfort? How does your faith and relationship with Christ help you to see beyond your needs?

3 When have you seen Christ in the people you've served? How so? What did they teach you? How were you changed by serving in that way?

4 How does knowing that caring for others is at the core of our calling as Christians push you to serve? How does your faith change the way you serve?

5 Where do you see suffering in your community? How can you step into those places and offer compassion and love?

Journal page

Journal page

Journal page

Journal page

Journal page

Journal page

Become a Friend of BRF Ministries
and give regularly to support our ministry

We help people of all ages to grow in faith

We encourage and support individual Christians and churches as they serve and resource the changing spiritual needs of communities today.

Through **Anna Chaplaincy**
we're enabling churches to provide
spiritual care to older people

Through **Living Faith**
we're nurturing faith and resourcing
lifelong discipleship

Through **Messy Church**
we're helping churches to reach out
to families

Through **Parenting for Faith**
we're supporting parents as they raise
their children in the Christian faith

Our ministry is only possible because of the generous support of individuals, churches, trusts and gifts in wills.

As we look to the future and make plans, **regular donations make a huge difference** in ensuring we can both start and finish projects well.

By becoming a Friend and giving regularly to our ministry, you are partnering with us in the gospel and helping change lives.

How your gift makes a difference

£2 a month
Helps us to give away **Living Faith** resources via food banks and chaplaincy services

£10 a month
Helps us to support parents and churches running the **Parenting for Faith** course

£5 a month
Helps us to support **Messy Church** volunteers and grow the wider network

£20 a month
Helps us to develop the reach of **Anna Chaplaincy** and improve spiritual care for older people

How to become a Friend of BRF Ministries

Online – set up a Direct Debit donation at **brf.org.uk/donate** or find out how to set up a Standing Order at **brf.org.uk/friends**

By post – complete and return the form opposite to 'Freepost BRF' (*no other address or stamp is needed*)

If you have any questions, or if you want to change your regular donation or stop giving in the future, do get in touch.

Contact the fundraising team

Email: **giving@brf.org.uk**
Tel: +44 (0)1235 462305
Post: Fundraising team, BRF Ministries,
         15 The Chambers, Vineyard,
         Abingdon OX14 3FE

Registered with

FR

FUNDRAISING **REGULATOR**

SHARING OUR VISION – MAKING A GIFT

I would like to make a donation to support BRF Ministries.
Please use my gift for:

☐ Where it is most needed ☐ Anna Chaplaincy ☐ Living Faith

☐ Messy Church ☐ Parenting for Faith

Title	First name/initials	Surname

Address	
	Postcode

Email

Telephone

Signature	Date

Please accept my gift of:

☐ £2 ☐ £5 ☐ £10 ☐ £20 Other £ _____

by (*delete as appropriate*):

☐ Cheque/Charity Voucher payable to 'BRF'

☐ MasterCard/Visa/Debit card/Charity card

Name on card

Card no. ☐☐☐☐ ☐☐☐☐ ☐☐☐☐ ☐☐☐☐

Expires end ☐M ☐M ☐Y ☐Y Security code* ☐☐☐ *Last 3 digits on the reverse of the card

Signature	Date

Please complete other side of this form

BRF Ministries Gift Aid Declaration

In order to Gift Aid your donation, you must tick the box below.

☐ I want to Gift Aid my donation and any donation I make in the future or have made in the past four years to BRF Ministries

I am a UK taxpayer and understand that if I pay less Income Tax and/or Capital Gains Tax in the current tax year than the amount of Gift Aid claimed on all my donations, it is my responsibility to pay any difference.

Please notify BRF Ministries if you want to cancel this Gift Aid declaration, change your name or home address, or no longer pay sufficient tax on your income and/or capital gains.

You can also give online at **brf.org.uk/donate**, which reduces our administration costs, making your donation go further.

Our ministry is only possible because of the generous support of individuals, churches, trusts and gifts in wills.

☐ I would like to leave a gift to BRF Ministries in my will.
   Please send me further information.

☐ I would like to find out about giving a regular gift to BRF Ministries.

For help or advice regarding making a gift, please contact our fundraising team +44 (0)1235 462305

Your privacy

We will use your personal data to process this transaction. From time to time we may send you information about the work of BRF Ministries that we think may be of interest to you. Our privacy policy is available at **brf.org.uk/privacy**. Please contact us if you wish to discuss your mailing preferences.

Registered with

FUNDRAISING
REGULATOR

⟲ Please complete other side of this form

Please return this form to 'Freepost BRF'
No other address information or stamp is needed

Bible Reading Fellowship is a charity (233280) and company limited by guarantee (301324), registered in England and Wales

UR0225

**Reimagining the
Landscape of Faith**
Essential pathways for spiritual growth

Is this all there is to faith? Every Christian carries a map, a mental image of their journey through life, created from their Christian tradition, their cultural background and their understanding of the Bible. Many Christians will also, at some point in their life, begin to question their map – causing them to ask, 'Is this all there is?' and 'How did I get here?' Mary and Charles Hippsley help us to identify our faith map, including the unexamined assumptions that underpin it. Then, drawing on a range of sources of wisdom, including personal experience, they gently encourage us to allow God to expand our map when we find that our faith doesn't match up with the reality of life.

Reimagining the Landscape of Faith
Essential pathways for spiritual growth
Mary and Charles Hippsley
978 1 80039 271 7 £12.99
brfonline.org.uk

What does 'All shall be well' mean when all is not well? Through revelations ten to sixteen of her *Revelations of Divine Love*, Julian of Norwich returns time and again to the idea that 'all is well', and Emma Pennington examines this popular mantra and explores what Julian really means by it, bringing depth and relevance to these words for the reader who lives in an age of pandemic, war and climate crisis which closely echoes Julian's own. Deep engagement with Julian's visions of salvation encourages the reader to reflect in prayer and devotion on their own personal relationship with God..

All Shall Be Well
Visions of salvation with Julian of Norwich
Emma Pennington
978 1 80039 206 9 £12.99
brfonline.org.uk

How to encourage Bible reading in your church

BRF Ministries has been helping individuals connect with the Bible for over 100 years. We want to support churches as they seek to encourage church members into regular Bible reading.

Order a Bible reading resources pack
This pack is designed to give your church the tools to publicise our Bible reading notes. It includes:

- Sample Bible reading notes for your congregation to try.
- Publicity resources, including a poster.
- A church magazine feature about Bible reading notes.

The pack is free, but we welcome a £5 donation to cover the cost of postage. If you require a pack to be sent outside the UK or require a specific number of sample Bible reading notes, please contact us for postage costs. For more information about what the current pack contains, go to **brfonline.org.uk/pages/bible-reading-resources-pack**.

How to order and find out more
- Email **enquiries@brf.org.uk**
- Phone us on +44 (0)1865 319700 Mon–Fri 9.30–17.00.
- Write to us at BRF Ministries, 15 The Chambers, Vineyard, Abingdon OX14 3FE.

Keep informed about our latest initiatives
We are continuing to develop resources to help churches encourage people into regular Bible reading, wherever they are on their journey. Join our email list at **brfonline.org.uk/signup** to stay informed about the latest initiatives that your church could benefit from.

Subscriptions

The Upper Room is published in January, May and September.

Individual subscriptions
The subscription rate for orders for 4 or fewer copies includes postage and packing:

The Upper Room annual individual subscription   £21.30

Group subscriptions
Orders for 5 copies or more, sent to ONE address, are post free:
The Upper Room annual group subscription   £15.75

Please do not send payment with order for a group subscription. We will send an invoice with your first order.

Please note that the annual billing period for group subscriptions runs from 1 May to 30 April.

Copies of the notes may also be obtained from Christian bookshops.

Single copies of *The Upper Room* cost £5.25.

Prices valid until 30 April 2026.

Giant print version
The Upper Room is available in giant print for the visually impaired, from:

Torch Trust for the Blind
Torch House
Torch Way
Northampton Road
Market Harborough   Tel: +44 (0)1858 438260
LE16 9HL   **torchtrust.org**

To set up a recurring subscription, please go to brfonline.org.uk/subscriptions

☐ I would like to take out a subscription myself (complete your name and address details once)

☐ I would like to give a gift subscription (please provide both names and addresses)

Title .... First name/initials .... Surname ....

Address ....

.... Postcode ....

Telephone .... Email ....

Gift subscription name ....

Gift subscription address ....

.... Postcode ....

Gift message (20 words max. or include your own gift card):

....

....

Please send *The Upper Room* beginning with the September 2025 / January 2026 / May 2026 issue (*delete as appropriate*):

Annual individual subscription ☐ £21.30

Optional donation* to support the work of BRF Ministries £ ....

Total enclosed £ .... (cheques should be made payable to 'BRF')

*Please complete and return the Gift Aid declaration on page 159 to make your donation even more valuable to us.

Method of payment

Please charge my MasterCard / Visa with £ ....

Card no. ☐☐☐☐ ☐☐☐☐ ☐☐☐☐ ☐☐☐☐

Expires end ☐☐ ☐☐   Security code ☐☐☐   Last 3 digits on the reverse of the card

To set up a recurring subscription, please go to brfonline.org.uk/subscriptions

☐ Please send me .... copies of *The Upper Room* September 2025 / January 2026 / May 2026 issue (*delete as appropriate*)

Title .... First name/initials .... Surname ....

Address ....

.... Postcode ....

Telephone .... Email ....

Please do not send payment with this order. We will send an invoice with your first order.

Christian bookshops: All good Christian bookshops stock our resources. For your nearest stockist, please contact us.

Telephone: The BRF office is open Mon–Fri 9.30–17.00. To place your order, telephone +44 (0)1865 319700.

Online: brfonline.org.uk/group-subscriptions

☐ Please send me a Bible reading resources pack to encourage Bible reading in my church

Please return this form with the appropriate payment to:
BRF Ministries, 15 The Chambers, Vineyard, Abingdon OX14 3FE

For terms and cancellation information, please visit **brfonline.org.uk/terms**.

Bible Reading Fellowship is a charity (233280) and company limited by guarantee (301324), registered in England and Wales